The Power of CMS

WordPress is important for most people because of the following reasons:

User-Friendly Interface: WordPress offers a user-friendly interface that makes it accessible to individuals without extensive technical knowledge. It allows users to create and manage websites without needing to learn complex coding or web development languages.

Content Management: WordPress is primarily a content management system (CMS), designed to handle the creation and organization of digital content. It provides intuitive tools for creating and publishing blog posts, pages, media, and other types of content.

Flexibility and Customization: WordPress offers a wide range of themes and plugins that allow users to customize the appearance and functionality of their websites. Themes provide pre-designed layouts and styling options, while plugins add specific features and functionality. This flexibility allows users to create unique and tailored websites to suit their needs.

Wide Range of Applications: WordPress is versatile and can be used for various types of websites, including blogs, personal portfolios, business websites, e-commerce stores, online communities, and more. Its extensive plugin ecosystem ensures that there are solutions available for different industry requirements and website goals.

SEO-Friendly: WordPress is built with search engine optimization (SEO) in mind. It generates clean and SEO-friendly code, making it easier for search engines to index and rank websites. Additionally, there are numerous SEO plugins available to optimize website content and improve visibility in search engine results.

Active Community and Support: WordPress has a large and active community of users, developers, designers, and contributors. This community provides support, resources, and documentation that help users troubleshoot issues, learn new skills, and stay updated with the latest developments in WordPress.

Scalability and Growth: WordPress is scalable and can accommodate websites of all sizes, from small personal blogs to large enterprise-level websites with high traffic. As businesses and websites grow, WordPress can handle increased demands and can be extended with additional features and functionalities.

Open-Source and Cost-Effective: WordPress is an open-source software, which means it is freely available to use, modify, and distribute. This makes it a cost-effective solution for individuals and businesses, as there is no need to pay licensing fees. Users have the freedom to customize and adapt WordPress to their specific needs without incurring significant expenses.

Overall, WordPress provides a powerful and accessible platform for individuals, businesses, and organizations to create and manage websites. Its ease of use, flexibility, and vast ecosystem of themes and plugins have made it a popular choice for most people looking to establish their online presence or enhance their digital capabilities.

Create A New Website With Wordpress

Hannah Milloch

CONTENTS

EASY WEBSITE CREATION

Are you ready to embark on an exciting journey into the world of website creation? Brace yourself, because we have some exciting news for you: "You don't need to be a professional to create a professional website!" In this groundbreaking book, Redel Gabster will guide you through the step-by-step process of building a stunning website that rivals the work of seasoned professionals. Get ready to unleash your creativity and showcase your unique vision to the world.

In "Unleash Your Creativity," Hannah Milloch empowers you to create a professional website without the need for professional experience. Through practical advice, easy-to-follow tutorials, and inspirational examples, you'll gain the confidence to turn your vision into a stunning reality. Get ready to embark on this transformative journey and leave your mark on the digital world.

Don't let the lack of professional experience hold you back. With "Unleash Your Creativity," you have the power to create a website that rivals the work of seasoned professionals. So, roll up your sleeves, let your creativity soar, and get ready to launch a website that leaves a lasting impression.

WORDPRESS

WordPress is a popular content management system (CMS) that allows you to create, manage, and publish content on the web. It provides a user-friendly interface, making it accessible for both beginners and experienced users. WordPress powers a significant portion of websites on the internet, ranging from personal blogs to e-commerce sites and corporate websites.

At its core, WordPress consists of two main components: the WordPress software (WordPress.org) and the WordPress.com hosting platform. WordPress.org is an open-source software that can be downloaded and installed on your own web server. It provides more flexibility and control over your website's customization, themes, and plugins. On the other hand, WordPress.com is a hosted platform where you can create and manage a website without the need for self-hosting.

WordPress uses a database to store your website's content, including posts, pages, media files, and settings. It separates the content (stored in the database) from the design (handled by themes) and functionality (handled by plugins). This modular structure allows you to change the appearance and extend the functionality of your website without affecting the underlying content.

Themes define the visual design and layout of your WordPress website. They control the appearance of your site, including colors, fonts, page structure, and other design elements. Themes can be customized or replaced to give your website a unique look and feel. There are thousands of free and premium themes available, catering to various industries and design preferences.

Plugins are additional software components that add specific features and functionality to your WordPress website. They can be used to enhance SEO, add contact forms, integrate e-commerce functionality, improve security, or extend the capabilities of your site in countless other ways. The WordPress plugin directory offers thousands of free plugins, and premium plugins are available from third-party developers.

Regarding security, WordPress has made significant improvements over the years to address vulnerabilities and ensure a secure environment. However, the security of your WordPress website ultimately depends on how you configure and maintain it. Here are some security best practices for WordPress:

Keep WordPress Updated: Regularly update your WordPress installation, themes, and plugins to ensure you have the latest security patches and bug fixes.

Use Strong Usernames and Passwords: Choose unique, strong passwords for your WordPress admin account and all user accounts associated with your website.

Install Security Plugins: Use reputable security plugins like Wordfence, Sucuri, or iThemes Security to strengthen your website's security. These plugins provide features such as malware scanning, firewall protection, and login protection.

Limit Login Attempts: Implement measures to prevent brute-force attacks by limiting the number of login attempts and enforcing strong password policies.

Regular Backups: Set up automated backups of your website's files and database to ensure you have a copy in case of any security incidents or data loss.

Secure Hosting Environment: Choose a reliable and secure hosting provider that employs security measures, including regular server and software updates, firewalls, and malware scanning.

Stay Informed: Keep yourself updated on the latest security practices, vulnerabilities, and recommended security measures for WordPress websites.

While WordPress provides a solid foundation for building secure websites, it's important to remain vigilant and follow security best practices to protect your site from potential threats.

MASTER CMS TO EMPOWER DESIGN:

In the world of website design, creativity is the key to standing out from the crowd. In this exciting chapter, we will delve into the realm of design and empower you to embrace your inner designer. You'll discover how to tap into your innate creativity, develop an eye for captivating design, and create visually stunning websites that leave a lasting impact on your visitors.

1. Understanding the Power of Design:

- Explore the importance of design in creating memorable user experiences.

- Learn how effective design can enhance your website's credibility and engagement.

2. Unleashing Your Creative Potential:

- Discover techniques to overcome creative blocks and unleash your unique vision.

- Explore exercises and practices to stimulate your creativity and think outside the box.

3. The Fundamentals of Visual Design:

- Dive into the principles of color theory, typography, and layout.

- Learn how to choose harmonious color palettes, select suitable fonts, and create balanced compositions.

4. Crafting Engaging User Interfaces:

- Explore the art of creating user-friendly and visually appealing interfaces.

- Understand the importance of intuitive navigation, clear calls-to-action, and effective use of whitespace.

5. Designing for Different Devices:

- Learn the principles of responsive design and how to create websites that adapt to different screen sizes.

- Understand the importance of mobile-friendly design and optimize your website for a seamless mobile experience.

6. Creating Compelling Visuals:

- Discover techniques for selecting and editing images that enhance your website's visual impact.

- Explore the world of graphics, illustrations, and icons to add personality and flair to your designs.

7. Iterative Design and User Feedback:

- Understand the value of iterating and refining your designs based on user feedback.

- Learn how to conduct user testing and gather valuable insights to improve your design decisions.

Embracing your inner designer is the key to unlocking your creative genius in website design. By understanding the power of design, unleashing your creativity, and mastering the fundamentals, you'll be equipped to create visually stunning websites that captivate your audience. In the next chapter, we will delve into the realm of user experience and learn how to create seamless and delightful interactions on your website. Get ready to transform your designs into unforgettable user experiences!

DISCOVER HOW TO TAP INTO YOUR INNATE CREATIVITY AND DEVELOP AN EYE FOR CAPTIVATING DESIGN.

In the vast realm of website design, creativity is the secret ingredient that sets exceptional websites apart. In this captivating chapter, we will embark on a journey to unlock your innate creativity and help you develop an eye for captivating design. By tapping into your artistic potential, you'll learn to create visually stunning websites that leave a lasting impression on your visitors.

1. Embracing Your Creative Spirit:

- Discover the power of creativity and its significance in website design.

- Unleash your imagination and embrace a mindset of curiosity and exploration.

2. Cultivating Inspiration:

- Explore techniques for finding inspiration in everyday life, from art and nature to architecture and fashion.

- Learn how to observe, collect, and document sources of inspiration to fuel your design process.

3. Nurturing Your Creative Process:

- Develop effective habits and routines that enhance your creativity.

- Experiment with brainstorming techniques, mind mapping, and mood boards to generate innovative ideas.

4. Exploring Design Principles:

- Delve into the fundamental principles of design, such as balance, harmony, contrast, and hierarchy.

- Learn how to apply these principles to your website designs to create visually pleasing compositions.

5. Developing a Design Sensibility:

- Train your eye to recognize and appreciate good design in various contexts.

- Analyze and critique existing websites, identifying their strengths and areas for improvement.

6. Keeping Up with Design Trends:

- Stay informed about the latest design trends and emerging styles.

- Understand how to incorporate current design trends into your website designs while maintaining a timeless appeal.

7. Practicing Design Exercises:

- Engage in hands-on design exercises to enhance your skills and creativity.

- Explore activities such as mood board creation, style exploration, and mockup design to sharpen your design sensibilities.

Conclusion: By tapping into your innate creativity and developing an eye for captivating design, you have the power to create visually stunning websites that leave a lasting impact. Embracing your inner designer is not just about following rules; it's about unleashing your unique perspective and expressing your creativity through thoughtful design choices. In the next chapter, we will delve into the practical aspects of designing user-friendly interfaces that ensure delightful experiences for your website visitors. Get ready to transform your ideas into captivating designs that inspire and engage!

COLOR THEORY, TYPOGRAPHY, AND LAYOUT TO CREATE VISUALLY STUNNING WEBSITES

In the realm of website design, understanding the fundamentals of color theory, typography, and layout is essential to create visually stunning and engaging websites. In this chapter, we will embark on a journey to master these key elements, enabling you to bring your designs to life with harmonious color schemes, captivating typography, and well-balanced layouts.

1. Exploring Color Theory:

- Understand the principles of color theory and how different colors evoke emotions and convey meaning.

- Learn about color harmonies, contrast, and the psychology of color to make informed design decisions.

2. Selecting a Color Palette:

- Discover techniques for choosing the perfect color palette that aligns with your website's purpose and brand identity.

- Explore color combinations and tools to create visually appealing and harmonious color schemes.

3. Typography: The Art of Beautiful Text:

- Dive into the world of typography and its impact on user experience and visual aesthetics.

- Learn about font families, font pairing, hierarchy, and readability to make typography choices that enhance your website's design.

4. Creating Effective Layouts:

- Understand the principles of visual hierarchy, grid systems, and whitespace to craft well-organized and balanced layouts.

- Learn about responsive design techniques to ensure your website looks great on various devices and screen sizes.

5. Enhancing User Experience with Visual Elements:

- Explore the use of images, icons, illustrations, and other visual elements to enhance the user experience and convey your message effectively.

- Understand the importance of visual consistency and how it contributes to the overall visual appeal of your website.

6. Designing for Accessibility:

- Learn about inclusive design principles and techniques to ensure your website is accessible to users of all abilities.

- Discover tools and guidelines for creating a user-friendly experience for individuals with visual impairments or other accessibility needs.

Conclusion: By mastering the fundamentals of color theory, typography, and layout, you gain the power to create visually stunning websites that captivate and engage your audience. Understanding the psychology of color, choosing harmonious color palettes, selecting appropriate typography, and crafting well-balanced layouts are essential skills for any aspiring web designer. In the next chapter, we will delve deeper into the art of user experience design and explore techniques to create intuitive and delightful interactions on your website. Get ready to take your designs to the next level and leave a lasting visual impact!

MASTERING USER EXPERIENCE:

In the world of website design, creating a seamless and delightful user experience (UX) is key to engaging and satisfying your visitors. In this immersive chapter, we will explore the art of mastering user experience, equipping you with the knowledge and techniques to craft websites that leave a lasting impact. Get ready to dive into the world of user-centric design and create websites that captivate and delight your audience.

1. Understanding User-Centered Design:

- Explore the core principles of user-centered design and its importance in creating exceptional websites.

- Learn to empathize with your users, identify their needs and goals, and design experiences that meet their expectations.

2. Conducting User Research:

- Dive into the world of user research and discover techniques for gathering valuable insights about your target audience.

- Explore methods such as surveys, interviews, and usability testing to uncover user preferences and pain points.

3. Creating Effective Information Architecture:

- Learn how to structure and organize your website's content in a way that is intuitive and easy to navigate.

- Discover techniques for creating clear navigation menus, logical page hierarchies, and user-friendly search functionalities.

4. Crafting Intuitive Interactions:

- Explore the art of interaction design and learn to create intuitive and seamless interactions on your website.

- Discover techniques for designing effective forms, implementing clear calls-to-action, and providing feedback to users.

5. Optimizing for Mobile and Responsive Design:

- Understand the importance of mobile-friendly design and how to optimize your website for various devices.

- Learn about responsive design techniques, flexible layouts, and adaptive images to provide a consistent experience across different screen sizes.

6. Enhancing Website Performance:

- Explore techniques for optimizing website performance to ensure fast loading times and smooth interactions.

- Learn about image optimization, caching, and code optimization to create a seamless browsing experience for your users.

7. Testing and Iterating:

- Understand the significance of user testing and feedback in improving your website's user experience.

- Learn how to conduct usability tests, analyze feedback, and iterate on your design to continuously enhance the user experience.

Conclusion: Mastering user experience is the key to creating exceptional websites that engage and delight your visitors. By understanding the principles of user-centered design, conducting user research, crafting intuitive interactions, and optimizing for mobile devices, you'll be equipped to create websites that leave a positive and lasting impression. In the next chapter, we will delve into the fascinating world of visual design, exploring techniques to create captivating aesthetics that complement your user-centered experiences. Get ready to take your website's user experience to new heights and create experiences that your users will love.

SEAMLESS USER EXPERIENCES THAT KEEP VISITORS ENGAGED AND DELIGHTED

In the world of website design, the art of crafting seamless user experiences is paramount to capturing and retaining the attention of your visitors. In this immersive chapter, we will explore the techniques and principles that will empower you to create user experiences that not only engage but also delight your audience. Get ready to embark on a journey into the captivating realm of user experience design.

1. Understanding User Experience Design:

- Explore the core concepts of user experience (UX) design and its impact on website success.

- Learn about the importance of empathy, understanding user goals, and creating delightful interactions.

2. User-Centric Design Principles:

- Discover the principles that guide user-centric design, such as simplicity, clarity, and consistency.

- Explore techniques for designing intuitive navigation, clear content hierarchy, and user-friendly interfaces.

3. Mapping User Journeys:

- Learn how to map out the user journey, from their initial visit to achieving their goals on your website.

- Explore techniques for identifying pain points, optimizing touchpoints, and ensuring a smooth flow of interactions.

4. Responsive and Mobile-Friendly Design:

- Understand the significance of responsive design and the need to provide a seamless experience across different devices.

- Learn techniques for optimizing your website for mobile devices, such as adaptive layouts and touch-friendly interactions.

5. Usability and Accessibility:

- Explore the principles of usability and accessibility in website design.

- Learn techniques for creating intuitive navigation, readable content, and inclusive experiences for all users.

6. Engaging Interactions and Microinteractions:

- Discover the art of designing engaging interactions that captivate your visitors.

- Learn about the power of microinteractions, such as animations, tooltips, and notifications, in enhancing user engagement.

7. Testing and Iterating for Continuous Improvement:

- Understand the importance of user testing and feedback in refining your user experiences.

- Explore techniques for conducting usability tests, gathering feedback, and iterating on your designs.

Conclusion: Crafting seamless user experiences is an art that requires a deep understanding of your audience, their goals, and the principles of user-centric design. By embracing empathy, simplicity, and clarity, you can create website experiences that engage and delight your visitors. In the next chapter, we will delve into the world of visual design, exploring techniques to enhance the aesthetics of your website and create visually captivating experiences. Get ready to transform your website into a delightful journey for your users, keeping them engaged and coming back for more.

NAVIGATION, READABILITY, AND INTERACTION TO CREATE AN INTUITIVE WEBSITE

In the digital landscape, creating an intuitive website is essential to provide a seamless and enjoyable user experience. In this enlightening chapter, we will explore techniques that will empower you to optimize navigation, readability, and interaction, resulting in a website that is intuitive and easy to use. Get ready to embark on a journey to create a user-friendly digital space that your visitors will love.

1. Streamlining Navigation:

- Learn how to design clear and intuitive navigation menus that guide users through your website.

- Explore techniques for organizing content, creating logical hierarchies, and implementing search functionality for easy exploration.

2. Enhancing Readability:

- Discover strategies to improve the readability of your website's content.

- Learn about typography choices, font sizes, line spacing, and contrast to create content that is easy on the eyes.

3. Optimizing Visual Hierarchy:

- Understand the importance of visual hierarchy in guiding users' attention and emphasizing important elements.

- Explore techniques for utilizing size, color, and placement to create a clear and structured visual hierarchy.

4. Utilizing Effective Calls-to-Action (CTAs):

- Learn how to design compelling and action-oriented CTAs that encourage user engagement.

- Explore techniques for creating visually appealing CTAs, optimizing placement, and crafting persuasive copy.

5. Incorporating Responsive Design:

- Understand the significance of responsive design and its role in creating an intuitive experience across various devices and screen sizes.

- Learn techniques to ensure your website adapts seamlessly to different devices, providing a consistent and user-friendly interface.

6. Leveraging Interactive Elements:

- Discover the power of interactive elements to engage users and enhance their experience.

- Explore techniques for incorporating animations, hover effects, sliders, and interactive forms to make your website more engaging and interactive.

7. Conducting User Testing and Feedback:

- Learn the importance of user testing and gathering feedback to validate your design decisions.

- Explore techniques for conducting usability tests, collecting user feedback, and iteratively improving your website based on user insights.

Conclusion: By optimizing navigation, readability, and interaction, you can create an intuitive website that guides users seamlessly through their journey. Implementing streamlined navigation, enhancing readability, and utilizing effective CTAs will empower your visitors to effortlessly explore and engage with your content. Additionally, embracing responsive design and interactive elements will further enhance the overall user experience. In the next chapter, we will dive into the world of content creation, where you will learn how to craft compelling and engaging content that resonates with your audience. Get ready to captivate your visitors and provide them with an intuitive digital experience they won't forget.

DEMYSTIFYING WEBSITE TECHNOLOGIES

In the dynamic world of web development, understanding the core technologies is crucial to create and maintain effective websites. In this enlightening chapter, we will demystify the essential website technologies, empowering you to navigate the digital landscape with confidence. Get ready to unravel the tools and technologies that drive web development and unlock your potential as a web creator.

1. Introduction to HTML:

- Discover the fundamental building block of the web, HTML (Hypertext Markup Language).

- Learn about the structure, syntax, and tags used to create the foundation of web pages.

2. Unveiling CSS:

- Dive into the world of CSS (Cascading Style Sheets) and its role in styling web pages.

- Explore selectors, properties, and values to customize the visual appearance of your website.

3. Exploring JavaScript:

- Understand the power of JavaScript and its ability to add interactivity and dynamic functionality to web pages.

- Learn about variables, functions, events, and DOM manipulation to bring your websites to life.

4. Introduction to Server-Side Technologies:

- Discover the basics of server-side technologies, such as PHP, Python, or Node.js.

- Understand their role in processing data, connecting with databases, and generating dynamic content.

5. Unraveling Content Management Systems (CMS):

- Explore the world of CMS platforms, such as WordPress, Joomla, or Drupal.

- Understand how CMSs simplify website creation and management through intuitive interfaces and pre-built functionalities.

6. Harnessing the Power of Frameworks and Libraries:

- Learn about popular web development frameworks like React, Angular, or Vue.js.

- Discover how these frameworks enhance productivity and provide powerful tools for building robust and scalable web applications.

7. Exploring Version Control Systems:

- Understand the importance of version control systems like Git in managing and tracking changes to your website's codebase.

- Learn about essential Git commands and workflows to collaborate effectively and maintain code integrity.

Conclusion: Demystifying website technologies is the key to unlocking your potential as a web developer. By understanding HTML, CSS, JavaScript, server-side technologies, CMS platforms, frameworks, and version control systems, you'll have a solid foundation to build upon. In the next chapter, we will delve into the world of content creation, where you'll learn how to craft compelling and engaging content that captivates your audience. Get ready to wield the power of website technologies and embark on your journey to create remarkable web experiences.

HTML, CSS, AND JAVASCRIPT

1. HTML (Hypertext Markup Language): HTML is the standard markup language used to create the structure and content of web pages. It consists of a series of tags that define the elements within a web page. HTML tags are enclosed in angle brackets ("<>" and "</>") and provide semantic meaning to the content. For example, the <h1> tag represents a heading, the <p> tag represents a paragraph, and the <img> tag represents an image.

2. CSS (Cascading Style Sheets): CSS is a stylesheet language that controls the presentation and visual styling of HTML elements on a web page. It allows you to specify the colors, fonts, layouts, and other visual properties of your website. CSS uses selectors to target specific HTML elements and apply styling rules to them. For example, you can use the selector "h1" to target all heading 1 elements and define their font size, color, and margins.

3. JavaScript: JavaScript is a high-level programming language that adds interactivity and dynamic functionality to web pages. It allows you to create scripts that can respond to user interactions, manipulate HTML elements, handle data, make network requests, and perform calculations. JavaScript is executed by web browsers, making it a powerful tool for creating interactive and dynamic web experiences.

4. Libraries and Frameworks: Libraries and frameworks are pre-written collections of code that provide additional

functionality and simplify the development process. For example, jQuery is a popular JavaScript library that simplifies DOM manipulation and provides a wide range of utility functions. Frameworks like React, Angular, and Vue.js offer comprehensive sets of tools and components for building complex web applications.

5. Cross-Browser Compatibility: Cross-browser compatibility refers to the ability of a website to function consistently and display correctly across different web browsers, such as Chrome, Firefox, Safari, and Internet Explorer. Since each browser may interpret HTML, CSS, and JavaScript differently, developers need to ensure their code adheres to web standards and works reliably across multiple platforms.

6. Web Standards: Web standards are a set of guidelines and specifications established by the World Wide Web Consortium (W3C) to ensure interoperability and accessibility of web content. Adhering to web standards helps create websites that are compatible with a wide range of devices, browsers, and assistive technologies. It also promotes best practices in terms of code quality, performance, and user experience.

By understanding and effectively utilizing these elements, web developers can create well-structured, visually appealing, and interactive websites that provide an exceptional user experience.

RESPONSIVE DESIGN

Responsive design is an approach to web design that aims to provide an optimal viewing and interaction experience across a wide range of devices and screen sizes. It ensures that your website adapts and responds to the user's device, whether it's a desktop computer, laptop, tablet, or smartphone. Here's how responsive design helps your website look amazing on any device:

1. Fluid Layouts: Responsive design uses fluid grids and flexible layouts that adjust proportionally to fit different screen sizes. This allows your website to expand or shrink, ensuring content is displayed appropriately without horizontal scrolling or content cutoff.

2. Media Queries: By using CSS media queries, you can apply different styles and layouts based on the characteristics of the user's device, such as screen width, height, orientation, and resolution. Media queries allow you to target specific device sizes and apply custom styles accordingly.

3. Flexible Images: Responsive design includes techniques for scaling images and media elements proportionally to fit different screen sizes. This prevents images from being too large or too small, ensuring they remain clear and visually appealing on any device.

4. Adaptive Typography: With responsive design, typography is adjusted based on the screen size. This means font sizes, line spacing, and other typographic elements adapt to provide optimal readability and legibility on different devices.

5. Touch-Friendly Interactions: Mobile devices primarily use touch-based interactions, and responsive design takes this into account. It ensures that buttons, links, and interactive

elements are appropriately sized and spaced to accommodate touch inputs, making the user experience seamless and intuitive on touchscreen devices.

6. Improved User Experience: Responsive design prioritizes user experience by eliminating the need for users to zoom in or scroll horizontally to view content. It ensures that your website is accessible, easy to navigate, and visually appealing, regardless of the device being used.

By implementing responsive design techniques, you can create a website that not only looks amazing but also delivers an exceptional user experience on any device. Whether your visitors are browsing on a large desktop monitor or a small smartphone screen, your website will adapt and provide an optimal viewing experience, increasing engagement, and ensuring your content is accessible to all users.

CONTENT CREATION STRATEGIES

In the fast-paced digital landscape, creating content that captivates and engages your audience is the key to standing out among the noise. In this chapter, we will explore content creation strategies that will empower you to craft compelling and engaging website content right from the start. By understanding your target audience, defining clear goals, and implementing effective techniques, you can create content that resonates with your readers and keeps them coming back for more.

1. Understanding Your Target Audience: To create content that truly connects with your audience, it is crucial to understand who they are and what they are looking for. Take the time to conduct audience research and create detailed buyer personas that represent your ideal website visitors. By understanding their demographics, motivations, pain points, and preferences, you can tailor your content to their specific needs and interests.

2. Defining Your Content Goals and Objectives: To ensure your content creation efforts are purposeful and aligned with your website strategy, it is essential to define clear goals and objectives. What do you want to achieve with your content? Is it to educate, entertain, inspire, or drive conversions? Set SMART goals (Specific, Measurable, Achievable, Relevant, Time-bound) that align with your overall website objectives, and keep them in mind as you create your content.

3. Crafting Attention-Grabbing Headlines and Introductions: The first impression matters, and in the digital world, it all starts with your headlines and introductions. Craft attention-grabbing headlines that are concise, descriptive, and entice readers to click and explore further. Follow up

with introductions that captivate and set the stage for the rest of your content. Hook your readers from the start and make them eager to delve deeper.

4. Structuring Engaging and Digestible Content: In today's fast-paced online environment, users prefer content that is easy to consume and understand. Structure your content in a way that is clear, organized, and easy to navigate. Use headings, subheadings, bullet points, and formatting techniques to break down information into digestible chunks. This not only enhances readability but also allows readers to scan and grasp the main points quickly.

5. Writing Compelling and Relatable Copy: Great content goes beyond delivering information; it connects with readers on an emotional level. Write copy that speaks to your audience's pain points, desires, and aspirations. Incorporate storytelling techniques, use persuasive language, and provide relevant examples to make your content relatable and memorable. Create a connection with your readers and leave a lasting impact.

6. Enhancing Content with Visuals and Multimedia: Visuals are powerful tools that can enhance the impact of your content. Incorporate high-quality images, videos, infographics, and interactive media to convey information in a visually appealing and engaging way. Visuals not only capture attention but also facilitate better understanding and information retention. Use them strategically to support and complement your written content.

7. Optimizing for Search Engines (SEO): To increase the discoverability of your content, it is important to optimize it for search engines. Conduct keyword research to understand the words and phrases your target audience is searching for. Incorporate relevant keywords naturally

throughout your content, including in headings, meta tags, and descriptions. This helps search engines understand the relevance of your content and improves its visibility in search results.

8. Encouraging Interaction and Engagement: Engaging your audience goes beyond just delivering content. Encourage interaction and engagement by allowing comments, providing social sharing options, and actively seeking user feedback. User-generated content, such as testimonials, reviews, and discussions, adds authenticity and fosters a sense of community. Actively participate in conversations and respond to comments to create a two-way dialogue with your readers.

Conclusion: Crafting compelling and engaging website content is a skill that can be mastered with the right strategies and techniques. By understanding your audience, setting clear goals, and implementing effective content creation practices, you can create content that truly resonates with your readers. Remember to keep your target audience in mind, deliver value, and establish an emotional connection. With these strategies in place, you are well-equipped to create content that captures attention, drives engagement, and delivers results.

COMPELLING CONTENT

Creating compelling content that resonates with your target audience is crucial for engaging and connecting with them. Here are some strategies to help you craft content that truly resonates:

1. Understand Your Target Audience: Gain a deep understanding of your target audience's demographics, interests, needs, and pain points. Conduct audience research, create buyer personas, and use analytics to gather insights. This understanding will guide your content creation process.

2. Address Their Needs and Pain Points: Create content that addresses the specific needs, challenges, and aspirations of your target audience. Identify their pain points and offer solutions, tips, or advice that can help them overcome those challenges. By providing valuable solutions, you position yourself as a trusted resource.

3. Tell Compelling Stories: Humans are wired for storytelling. Craft narratives that resonate emotionally with your audience. Use real-life examples, personal experiences, and anecdotes to connect with them on a deeper level. Stories evoke emotions and make your content more relatable and memorable.

4. Use Clear and Conversational Language: Avoid jargon and complex terms that may alienate your audience. Use language that is simple, conversational, and easy to understand. Write in a tone that matches your brand's personality and resonates with your audience's preferences.

5. Provide Unique and Valuable Insights: Offer unique perspectives, insights, or knowledge that sets your content

apart. Share industry trends, research findings, or expert opinions that your audience may not find elsewhere. This positions you as an authority in your niche and gives readers a reason to keep coming back for more.

6. Use Engaging Formats: Experiment with different content formats to keep your audience engaged. Incorporate visuals, such as images, infographics, or videos, to enhance the visual appeal of your content. Consider using interactive elements, such as quizzes, polls, or surveys, to encourage active participation.

7. Encourage Interaction and Feedback: Foster a sense of community by encouraging your audience to interact with your content. Pose questions, ask for opinions, and respond to comments. Create opportunities for dialogue and make your audience feel heard and valued.

8. Tailor Content to Different Channels: Adapt your content to the specific platforms or channels where your audience is active. Consider the characteristics of each platform, such as character limits on social media or visual-focused content on Instagram. Tailor your content to maximize its impact on each platform.

9. Continuously Monitor and Refine: Pay attention to the performance of your content. Analyze metrics such as engagement, shares, comments, and conversions. Use this data to identify what resonates best with your audience and refine your content strategy accordingly.

Remember, compelling content resonates when it genuinely speaks to the needs and interests of your target audience. By understanding them, addressing their pain points, telling engaging stories, and continuously refining your approach, you can create content that captures their attention, establishes trust, and builds a loyal following.

STORYTELLING

To create compelling content that captivates your visitors, consider incorporating storytelling, visuals, and persuasive copywriting techniques. Here's how you can leverage these elements:

1. Storytelling: Storytelling is a powerful tool for engaging your audience and creating an emotional connection. Craft narratives that resonate with your visitors by sharing relatable experiences, anecdotes, or case studies. Use storytelling to illustrate how your product or service solves problems, fulfills desires, or improves lives. Engage your audience's imagination and make them feel personally connected to your content.

2. Visuals: Visual elements can significantly enhance the impact of your content. Incorporate high-quality images, infographics, videos, and other visual media to support your message. Visuals not only make your content more visually appealing but also help convey information more effectively. Use captivating visuals that are relevant to your content and reinforce your key points. This will grab your visitors' attention and encourage them to explore further.

3. Persuasive Copywriting: Persuasive copywriting involves using language and techniques that influence and convince your audience. Use compelling headlines and introductions to hook your visitors from the start. Clearly communicate the benefits and value of your product or service, focusing on how it solves their problems or meets their needs. Employ persuasive language, such as powerful verbs, emotional triggers, and vivid descriptions, to engage and persuade your visitors to take action.

4. Use Engaging Formats: Experiment with different content formats to keep your visitors engaged. For instance, you

can create interactive quizzes, polls, or assessments that encourage active participation. Incorporate storytelling techniques in your blog posts, articles, or case studies to make them more engaging. Consider using multimedia formats, such as podcasts or videos, to provide dynamic and immersive experiences for your visitors.

5. Tailor Content to Your Audience: Understand your target audience and tailor your content to their preferences and interests. Conduct research, gather insights, and analyze user feedback to identify what resonates most with your visitors. Customize your storytelling, visuals, and copywriting style to match their needs and expectations. By understanding your audience's motivations, challenges, and aspirations, you can create content that truly speaks to them.

6. Test and Iterate: Continuously monitor the performance of your content and gather feedback from your visitors. Analyze metrics such as engagement rates, time on page, and conversion rates. Use A/B testing to experiment with different storytelling approaches, visual styles, and copywriting techniques. Based on the data and feedback, refine and optimize your content to better captivate and resonate with your audience.

By incorporating storytelling, visuals, and persuasive copywriting techniques, you can create content that captivates your visitors, sparks their interest, and compels them to take action. Remember to align these elements with your brand's voice, values, and goals to create a cohesive and impactful content strategy.

DIY WEBSITE DEVELOPMENT TOOLS

1. WordPress: A versatile and popular content management system (CMS) that allows you to create and manage websites with ease. It offers a wide range of themes, plugins, and customization options.

2. Wix: An intuitive drag-and-drop website builder that enables you to create visually appealing websites without any coding knowledge. It offers a variety of templates and features for different types of websites.

3. Squarespace: A comprehensive website builder known for its elegant designs and user-friendly interface. It provides customizable templates, built-in SEO tools, and reliable hosting services.

4. Weebly: A beginner-friendly website builder that offers a simple drag-and-drop editor and a wide selection of templates. It also provides e-commerce features, blogging capabilities, and domain registration.

5. Shopify: A popular platform specifically designed for creating and managing online stores. It offers a user-friendly interface, secure hosting, customizable templates, and a range of e-commerce features.

6. Joomla: A powerful open-source CMS that allows you to build complex websites with advanced functionality. It offers a flexible framework, extensive extensions, and a strong developer community.

7. Drupal: Another robust open-source CMS that provides advanced features for building complex websites. It is

highly customizable and suitable for large-scale projects that require scalability and security.

8. Magento: A feature-rich e-commerce platform that empowers businesses to create and manage online stores. It offers extensive customization options, strong SEO capabilities, and a dedicated community.

9. GoDaddy Website Builder: A simple and affordable website builder that caters to beginners. It provides pre-designed templates, a drag-and-drop editor, and reliable hosting services.

10. Jimdo: A user-friendly website builder that offers a range of templates and customization options. It includes e-commerce features, blogging capabilities, and mobile optimization.

11. Webflow: A professional website design and development tool that allows you to create visually stunning and responsive websites. It offers a visual editor, CMS capabilities, and advanced design options.

12. Elementor: A popular WordPress plugin that enhances the design and functionality of your website. It provides a drag-and-drop editor, pre-designed templates, and a wide range of widgets.

13. Google Sites: A free and simple website builder offered by Google. It allows you to create basic websites with easy collaboration features and integration with other Google services.

14. Bootstrap: A front-end framework that provides a collection of CSS and JavaScript components for building responsive websites. It offers a grid system, pre-styled components, and mobile-first design principles.

15. Adobe Dreamweaver: A professional web development tool that combines a visual editor with a code editor. It allows you to create and edit HTML, CSS, and JavaScript code while providing design and layout capabilities.

16. GitHub Pages: A free hosting service offered by GitHub that allows you to publish static websites directly from your GitHub repository. It is ideal for hosting documentation sites or personal portfolios.

17. Site123: A beginner-friendly website builder that offers a simple and intuitive interface. It provides pre-designed templates, SEO tools, and multilingual support.

18. Zoho Sites: A website builder that offers a range of templates, a drag-and-drop editor, and integration with other Zoho applications. It is suitable for small businesses and professionals.

19. Mobirise: A free offline website builder that enables you to create responsive websites without any coding. It offers a wide selection of templates and allows you to publish your site anywhere.

20. Constant Contact Website Builder: A user-friendly website builder that focuses on simplicity and ease of use. It offers drag-and-drop functionality, customizable templates, and e-commerce features.

21. Strikingly: A website builder specifically designed for creating single-page websites. It offers sleek templates, a mobile-responsive interface, and built-in e-commerce capabilities.

22. Ucraft: A modern website builder that provides a drag-and-drop editor, customizable templates, and integration with

third-party tools. It offers e-commerce features and multilingual support.

23. Square Online: A website builder that focuses on creating online stores. It offers easy inventory management, payment processing, and integration with Square's point-of-sale system.

24. Carrd: A simple and minimalistic website builder that allows you to create single-page websites. It is ideal for personal portfolios, landing pages, and small projects.

25. Tilda: A website builder that emphasizes visual storytelling and design. It offers a variety of templates, pre-designed blocks, and integration with popular marketing tools.

26. PageCloud: A flexible website builder that combines drag-and-drop functionality with advanced customization options. It offers a wide range of design elements and integrations.

27. GoDaddy Managed WordPress: A hosting platform specifically optimized for WordPress websites. It provides automatic updates, enhanced security, and reliable performance.

28. Joomla.com: A simplified version of Joomla that offers a user-friendly interface and hosting services. It is suitable for small websites and beginners.

29. Ghost: A lightweight CMS specifically designed for blogging. It offers a simple and distraction-free writing experience and focuses on speed and simplicity.

30. Google Sites: A free website builder provided by Google that allows you to create basic websites with easy collaboration features. It is suitable for simple informational sites or team projects.

31. Tumblr: A microblogging platform that combines blogging and social networking. It is popular for its simplicity and ease of use.

32. Medium: A content publishing platform that allows you to share your stories and articles with a large community of readers. It focuses on simplicity and readability.

33. WordPress.com: A hosted version of WordPress that provides an all-in-one solution for creating and managing websites. It offers a simplified interface, hosting, and support.

34. Blogger: A free blogging platform owned by Google. It allows you to create and publish blog posts easily and offers customization options.

35. Substack: A platform that enables you to create and monetize newsletters. It provides tools for building an email subscriber base and delivering content directly to subscribers' inboxes.

36. Ghost Pro: A hosted version of the Ghost CMS that provides a simplified and managed solution for publishing and managing content. It offers reliable hosting, regular backups, and support.

37. Webnode: A website builder that offers a drag-and-drop editor, customizable templates, and multilingual support. It is suitable for small businesses, portfolios, and personal websites.

38. Duda: A website builder that focuses on mobile responsiveness and offers a range of responsive templates. It provides advanced design and customization options.

39. Shopify Lite: A budget-friendly option for selling products or services online. It allows you to integrate a "Buy" button into your existing website or blog.

40. Odoo: An open-source business management software that includes a website builder among its many features. It offers e-commerce capabilities, CRM, and other business tools.

41. 1&1 IONOS Website Builder: A website builder that offers a range of templates, drag-and-drop functionality, and hosting services. It is suitable for small businesses and personal websites.

42. SiteBuilder: A website builder that provides drag-and-drop functionality, customizable templates, and e-commerce features. It offers a user-friendly interface for beginners.

43. Volusion: An e-commerce platform that provides a website builder, hosting, and online store management features. It offers customizable templates and integration with popular payment gateways.

44. GoDaddy Online Store: A platform that allows you to create an online store with ease. It provides design tools, payment processing, and inventory management features.

45. WooCommerce: A popular e-commerce plugin for WordPress that allows you to transform your WordPress website into an online store. It provides a wide range of customization options and extensions.

46. Ecwid: An e-commerce platform that offers seamless integration with existing websites or social media platforms. It provides a feature-rich shopping cart and various payment options.

47. PrestaShop: An open-source e-commerce platform that provides a comprehensive set of tools for creating and managing online stores. It offers a wide range of customization options and integrations.

48. BigCommerce: An e-commerce platform that caters to businesses of all sizes. It provides a comprehensive set of features, including hosting, design customization, and payment integration.

49. OpenCart: An open-source e-commerce platform that offers a user-friendly interface and a wide range of extensions. It is suitable for small to medium-sized online stores.

50. X-Cart: An e-commerce platform that provides a self-hosted solution for building online stores. It offers a robust set of features, including product management, payment integration, and marketing tools.

USER-FRIENDLY WEBSITE BUILDERS

1. WordPress: A versatile and widely-used content management system (CMS) that offers a user-friendly interface and a vast ecosystem of themes, plugins, and resources. It allows you to create and manage websites without extensive technical knowledge.

2. Wix: A popular website builder known for its intuitive drag-and-drop editor and user-friendly interface. It provides a wide range of templates, customization options, and built-in features that simplify the website development process.

3. Squarespace: A user-friendly website builder that offers visually stunning templates and a simple drag-and-drop interface. It provides integrated hosting, domain registration, and a range of built-in features for creating professional websites.

4. Weebly: A beginner-friendly website builder that offers a straightforward drag-and-drop editor and a wide selection of pre-designed templates. It allows you to customize your website easily and offers features like e-commerce integration and blogging capabilities.

5. Shopify: An e-commerce platform that simplifies the process of building online stores. It provides user-friendly tools for creating product listings, managing inventory, and processing payments. Shopify offers customizable themes and a seamless checkout experience.

6. Joomla: A user-friendly CMS that offers a visually appealing and intuitive interface. It provides flexible content management capabilities and a wide range of extensions and templates for building websites.

7. Drupal: A powerful CMS with a user-friendly interface that allows you to create and manage complex websites with ease. It offers extensive customization options, advanced content management features, and a robust developer community.

8. Magento: An e-commerce platform designed for businesses of all sizes. It offers a user-friendly interface, comprehensive product management features, and advanced customization options for building and scaling online stores.

9. GoDaddy Website Builder: A beginner-friendly website builder that simplifies the process of creating a professional website. It provides a simple drag-and-drop editor, customizable templates, and reliable hosting services.

10. Jimdo: A user-friendly website builder that offers an intuitive interface and a range of customizable templates. It provides easy-to-use design tools, SEO optimization features, and e-commerce capabilities.

11. Webflow: A visual web design and development platform that offers a user-friendly interface and powerful customization options. It allows you to design and build professional websites without writing code.

12. Elementor: A popular WordPress plugin that adds a user-friendly drag-and-drop editor to the platform. It simplifies the process of designing and customizing websites, allowing you to create visually appealing layouts without coding.

13. Google Sites: A simple and user-friendly website builder offered by Google. It allows you to create basic websites with easy collaboration features and integration with other Google services.

14. Shopify Lite: A simplified version of Shopify that allows you to add e-commerce functionality to an existing website or blog. It offers an easy-to-use interface for managing products and processing payments.

15. Carrd: A minimalist and user-friendly website builder that focuses on creating single-page websites. It provides a straightforward interface and customizable templates for creating simple and elegant sites.

These user-friendly website builders and CMS platforms simplify the website development process, making it accessible to individuals with varying levels of technical expertise. They provide intuitive interfaces, pre-designed templates, and built-in features that streamline the creation of professional and functional websites. Whether you're a beginner or an experienced developer, these tools empower you to bring your ideas to life without the need for extensive coding knowledge.

PLUGINS AND EXTENSIONS

1. Yoast SEO: A popular WordPress plugin that helps optimize your website for search engines. It provides tools for on-page SEO analysis, keyword optimization, XML sitemap generation, and more.

2. WooCommerce: A powerful e-commerce plugin for WordPress that enables you to create and manage an online store. It offers features such as product listings, shopping cart functionality, payment gateway integration, and order management.

3. Jetpack: A comprehensive plugin for WordPress that offers a suite of powerful features, including website security, performance optimization, social sharing, and content management tools.

4. WPForms: A user-friendly form builder plugin for WordPress that allows you to create custom forms without any coding. It offers a drag-and-drop interface, pre-built form templates, and advanced form field options.

5. Elementor: A versatile page builder plugin for WordPress that allows you to design and customize your website pages using a drag-and-drop interface. It offers a wide range of pre-designed templates and widgets for creating visually stunning layouts.

6. Akismet: A plugin that helps protect your website from spam comments. It automatically detects and filters spam comments, keeping your site clean and improving user experience.

7. Smush: An image optimization plugin for WordPress that helps reduce the file size of your images without compromising quality. It improves website performance by making your pages load faster.

8. WP Rocket: A caching plugin for WordPress that improves website speed and performance. It enables caching, file compression, and lazy loading of images, resulting in faster page load times.

9. Contact Form 7: A popular contact form plugin for WordPress that allows you to easily create and manage contact forms on your website. It offers customizable form fields, spam protection, and email notifications.

10. MonsterInsights: A Google Analytics plugin for WordPress that simplifies the integration and tracking of website analytics. It provides valuable insights into your website's traffic, user behavior, and conversions.

11. All in One SEO Pack: Another comprehensive SEO plugin for WordPress that helps optimize your website for search engines. It offers features such as XML sitemap generation, meta tag optimization, social media integration, and more.

12. WP Super Cache: A caching plugin for WordPress that generates static HTML files of your website, reducing server load and improving page load times. It helps enhance website performance and user experience.

13. Redirection: A plugin that allows you to manage 301 redirects and track 404 errors on your WordPress website. It helps maintain proper website structure and improves SEO.

14. UpdraftPlus: A backup plugin for WordPress that enables you to schedule and automate backups of your website's

files and database. It provides peace of mind by ensuring that you can easily restore your website in case of any data loss.

15. Social Snap: A social media sharing plugin that allows you to add social sharing buttons to your website's content. It offers customizable designs, social analytics, and integration with various social media platforms.

16. WPML: A plugin for creating multilingual websites with WordPress. It allows you to translate your website's content into multiple languages, making it accessible to a broader audience.

17. Wordfence Security: A comprehensive security plugin for WordPress that helps protect your website from malware, hacking attempts, and other security threats. It offers features such as firewall protection, malware scanning, and login security.

18. Advanced Custom Fields: A plugin that allows you to add custom fields to your WordPress website, giving you greater flexibility in content creation and customization.

19. Broken Link Checker: A plugin that scans your website for broken links and notifies you of any broken links found. It helps improve user experience and maintain good SEO practices.

20. WP Optimize: A plugin that helps optimize your WordPress database by removing unnecessary data, such as spam comments, revisions, and expired transients. It improves website performance and reduces database size.

These handy plugins and extensions add powerful features and functionality to your website without requiring any coding knowledge. They enhance your website's SEO, security, performance, user experience, and customization options, allowing you to create a professional and feature-rich website with ease.

OPTIMIZING FOR SEARCH ENGINES

Optimizing your website for search engines is crucial for improving its visibility and driving organic traffic. Here are some key strategies to optimize your website for search engines:

1. Keyword Research: Conduct thorough keyword research to identify relevant keywords and phrases that your target audience is searching for. Use keyword research tools to determine search volume, competition, and keyword variations. Incorporate these keywords strategically into your website's content, including page titles, headings, URLs, and meta descriptions.

2. On-Page Optimization: Optimize your website's individual pages for search engines. Ensure that your page titles, headings, and content include relevant keywords. Optimize your meta descriptions, URL structures, and image alt tags. Create unique and compelling content that provides value to your audience while incorporating relevant keywords naturally.

3. Quality Content Creation: Create high-quality, informative, and engaging content that is relevant to your target audience. Regularly update your website with fresh and valuable content, such as blog posts, articles, videos, or infographics. Focus on creating content that answers common questions, solves problems, or provides valuable insights to attract and engage your audience.

4. Mobile-Friendly Design: With the increasing use of mobile devices, it's crucial to ensure your website is mobile-friendly. Implement responsive design to ensure your website displays properly on various devices and screen sizes. Optimize page load times, as faster-loading websites

tend to rank higher in search results. Use mobile-friendly plugins or themes to enhance the mobile experience.

5. User Experience (UX): Enhance the overall user experience of your website. Ensure it has intuitive navigation, clear calls-to-action, and easy-to-use menus. Optimize your website's structure, making it easy for users and search engines to understand the hierarchy and flow of your content. Provide a positive user experience by focusing on page speed, accessibility, and easy-to-read content.

6. Link Building: Earn high-quality backlinks from reputable and relevant websites to improve your website's authority and visibility. Develop a link-building strategy that includes guest blogging, influencer outreach, and content promotion. Focus on acquiring natural and organic backlinks rather than resorting to spammy link-building tactics.

7. Social Media Integration: Integrate social media into your website to enhance your online presence and increase visibility. Encourage social sharing of your content, as it can lead to increased exposure and potential backlinks. Engage with your audience on social media platforms, respond to comments, and encourage user-generated content.

8. Technical SEO: Pay attention to technical aspects of your website that affect its search engine visibility. Optimize your website's crawlability and indexability by creating an XML sitemap, submitting it to search engines, and using robots.txt files. Ensure proper URL structures, canonical tags, and schema markup. Optimize your website's meta tags, headers, and alt tags.

9. Analyze and Improve: Continuously monitor and analyze your website's performance using tools like Google

Analytics and Google Search Console. Track important metrics such as organic traffic, keyword rankings, bounce rates, and conversions. Use the insights to identify areas of improvement and make data-driven decisions to optimize your website further.

By implementing these SEO strategies, you can improve your website's visibility in search engine results, attract more targeted organic traffic, and ultimately increase your chances of reaching your target audience. Remember that SEO is an ongoing process, so regularly monitor, adapt, and refine your approach to stay ahead of the competition and achieve long-term success.

ORGANIC TRAFFIC

Search engine optimization (SEO) is a crucial strategy for attracting organic traffic to your website. By optimizing your website and its content, you can improve your search engine rankings and increase visibility to potential visitors. Here are key steps to optimize your website for search engines:

1. Keyword Research: Conduct thorough keyword research to identify relevant keywords and phrases that your target audience is searching for. Use keyword research tools to find high-ranking keywords with moderate competition. Incorporate these keywords strategically into your website's content.

2. On-Page Optimization: Optimize your website's on-page elements to make them search engine-friendly. This includes optimizing meta tags (title tags, meta descriptions), using descriptive URLs, and incorporating relevant keywords naturally into your content.

3. Quality Content: Create high-quality, valuable content that is relevant to your target audience. Focus on providing informative and engaging content that answers their questions, solves their problems, or fulfills their needs. Use relevant keywords naturally within your content, but avoid keyword stuffing.

4. Site Structure and Navigation: Ensure your website has a clear and logical structure, making it easy for both users and search engines to navigate. Use a clear hierarchy, organize content into categories, and create a user-friendly menu and internal linking structure.

5. Mobile Optimization: With the increasing use of mobile devices, it's crucial to have a mobile-friendly website.

Optimize your website for mobile devices by using responsive design, ensuring fast page load times, and providing a seamless user experience across different screen sizes.

6. Page Speed Optimization: Improve your website's loading speed to enhance the user experience and search engine rankings. Optimize images, minify CSS and JavaScript files, use caching techniques, and choose a reliable web hosting provider to ensure fast loading times.

7. Link Building: Build high-quality backlinks from reputable websites to increase your website's authority and credibility. Focus on obtaining natural and relevant backlinks through guest blogging, social media sharing, influencer collaborations, and industry directories.

8. Social Media Integration: Integrate social media sharing buttons into your website's content to encourage users to share your content on social platforms. This can increase visibility and attract more organic traffic to your website.

9. Regular Content Updates: Keep your website fresh and up to date by regularly adding new content, updating existing content, and removing outdated information. Search engines favor websites that provide fresh and relevant content.

10. Monitor and Analyze: Use analytics tools to monitor your website's performance, track keyword rankings, and gain insights into user behavior. Analyze the data to identify areas for improvement and make data-driven decisions for your SEO strategy.

Remember, SEO is an ongoing process that requires continuous optimization, monitoring, and adaptation to changes in search engine algorithms. By implementing these strategies and staying up to date with SEO best practices, you can improve your website's visibility, attract organic traffic, and grow your online presence.

BEST PRACTICES

Boosting search rankings requires effective keyword research, on-page optimization, and link building. Here are some best practices for each:

1. Keyword Research:

   o Identify relevant keywords: Use keyword research tools to find keywords that align with your website's content and are frequently searched by your target audience.

   o Focus on long-tail keywords: Long-tail keywords are more specific and have less competition, allowing you to target a niche audience.

   o Consider search intent: Understand the intent behind the keywords and create content that aligns with what users are looking for.

   o Analyze competitor keywords: Research keywords your competitors are ranking for and identify opportunities to target similar terms.

2. On-Page Optimization:

   o Optimize meta tags: Craft compelling title tags and meta descriptions that include relevant keywords and entice users to click.

   o Incorporate keywords naturally: Place keywords strategically throughout your content, including in headings, subheadings, and within the body text.

   o Optimize URL structure: Use clean and descriptive URLs that include relevant keywords.

- o   Improve page load speed: Optimize image sizes, minify CSS and JavaScript files, and leverage caching to improve page load times.

  - o   Use header tags: Structure your content using header tags (H1, H2, H3) to improve readability and signal the importance of your content to search engines.

3. Link Building:

  - o   Focus on quality over quantity: Build links from reputable and authoritative websites within your industry or niche.

  - o   Earn natural backlinks: Create high-quality content that others find valuable and shareable, increasing the likelihood of earning organic backlinks.

  - o   Guest blogging: Contribute guest posts to relevant and authoritative websites, including a link back to your website in the author bio or content body.

  - o   Social media promotion: Share your content on social media platforms to increase its visibility and encourage others to link to it.

  - o   Monitor and disavow toxic links: Regularly check your backlink profile and disavow any low-quality or spammy links that may negatively impact your search rankings.

Remember, SEO is an ongoing process, and it's important to stay updated with the latest best practices and algorithm changes. Continuously monitor your website's performance, adapt your strategies as needed, and focus on providing valuable content that meets the needs of your target audience.

WEBSITE GLOBAL GROWTH

In today's digital landscape, the sheer number of websites being launched each year is staggering. With approximately 54 million websites entering the online realm annually, the challenge of maintaining visibility amidst the vast online competition is becoming increasingly difficult. Young websites often face an uphill battle as they strive to establish their presence and compete against well-established, highly ranked competitors.

The struggle to remain visible among the giants of the web, those websites with expansive indexed content and consistently high rankings, has led many users to seek out alternative approaches that are less time-consuming yet more effective. The need for innovative strategies that can yield quicker and more impactful results is more pressing than ever.

In this rapidly evolving digital landscape, it is essential for website owners and marketers to adapt and employ smart tactics to stay ahead of the competition. While building a successful online presence requires effort and time, there are approaches that can help accelerate the visibility and growth of your website.

By implementing targeted search engine optimization (SEO) techniques, crafting engaging and shareable content, and leveraging the power of social media and online advertising, you can boost your website's visibility and attract a larger audience. Additionally, staying up to date with the latest trends and algorithm changes, continuously monitoring and optimizing your website's performance, and cultivating meaningful connections within your industry or niche can further enhance your chances of success.

Remember, in this vast digital landscape, it's not just about launching a website; it's about implementing effective strategies that allow you to stand out, connect with your target audience, and rise above the competition. With the right combination of dedication, creativity, and strategic thinking, you can navigate the challenges of visibility and carve out your own space in the online world.

EFFICIENT KEYWORD RESEARCH

Effective keyword research is a vital step in optimizing your website for search engines. By investing just 5-20 minutes of your time, you can discover relevant keywords that will improve your website's visibility and attract targeted traffic. Follow these steps to conduct efficient keyword research using the Google Keyword Planner:

1. Visit the Google Keyword Planner website at https://adwords.google.com/KeywordPlanner and sign in with your Google account. If you don't have an account, you can create one for free.

2. Once you're logged in, you'll be directed to the main dashboard. On the left side of the page, click on "Search for new keyword and ad group ideas."

3. In the "Your product or service" box, enter a topic or word that accurately describes your website. This could be a broad topic related to your niche or a specific keyword you want to target.

4. Click on the blue "Get ideas" button and patiently wait for the page to load. The tool will analyze your input and generate a list of relevant keyword ideas.

5. On the next page, you'll see a range of keyword suggestions along with their average monthly search volume and other metrics. By default, the list is sorted by relevance, but you can click on "Avg. monthly searches" to see the keywords with the highest search volume at the top.

6. Scan through the keyword ideas and look for terms that align closely with your website's content and audience. Pay attention to the average monthly search volume to gauge the popularity of each keyword.

7. Aim for keywords that have more than 5,000 monthly searches as they indicate a significant level of interest. However, consider the relevance and competition level of each keyword as well. It's often beneficial to choose a mix of high-volume and niche-specific keywords.

8. As you find suitable keywords, make a note of them. Aim to compile a list of at least ten keywords that accurately represent your website and cover different aspects of your content.

Remember, the Google Keyword Planner is a powerful tool that can provide valuable insights into popular search terms related to your website. By investing a short amount of time in this keyword research process, you can lay a strong foundation for your search engine optimization efforts and increase your chances of ranking well in search results.

Keep in mind that keyword research is an ongoing process, and it's important to regularly evaluate and update your keyword strategy to stay relevant and adapt to changing search trends.

SELECTING A MEMORABLE WEBSITE DOMAIN NAME

Choosing the right domain name for your website is a crucial step in building your online presence. A memorable domain name not only represents your brand but also helps visitors easily find and remember your website. Here's a step-by-step process to quickly select a domain name that aligns with your content:

1. Visit a reputable domain registrar website such as www.namecheap.com or www.godaddy.com. These platforms offer user-friendly search tools and domain registration services.

2. In the search box located in the middle of the screen, enter a keyword or a cool word that accurately represents the essence of your website. Think about words or phrases that are relevant, catchy, and easy to remember. For example, if your website is about travel tips, consider keywords like "wanderlust" or "adventure".

3. Click on the search or enter button to initiate the domain search. The registrar's system will check the availability of your chosen domain name across different domain extensions, including the popular .com, .net, and .org.

4. Explore the search results to see which domain names are available. If your desired domain name is taken, the registrar websites often provide suggestions for alternative domain names or variations that may be available. Consider these suggestions and choose a name that closely aligns with your website's purpose.

5. Pay attention to the domain extension, as .com is generally preferred due to its widespread recognition and credibility. However, if you intend to target a specific country,

consider using the country-specific domain extension relevant to your audience. You can refer to websites like http://en.wikipedia.org/wiki/List_of_Internet_top-level_domains to find country-specific domain extensions.

6. Once you've found an available domain name that you're satisfied with, click on it to proceed with the registration process. This will typically take you to a page where you can review the details of your selection and choose additional services like privacy protection or SSL certificates if needed.

7. Create an account on the registrar website if you haven't already. Provide your contact information, including your name, email address, and billing details, to complete the registration process.

8. Before finalizing the registration, carefully review the domain name to ensure that it is spelled correctly and accurately represents your website. Once you're satisfied, proceed with the payment to secure the domain name for the specified duration, usually a year.

By investing just 5-10 minutes in selecting a memorable domain name, you'll be on your way to establishing a strong online identity. A well-chosen domain name can enhance your brand recognition, attract visitors, and contribute to the success of your website. Remember to renew your domain registration before it expires to maintain continuous access to your website and protect your online presence.

Keep in mind that selecting a domain name is a creative and strategic process. Experiment with different combinations of words, consider your target audience, and aim for a name that reflects your website's purpose and resonates with your visitors.

SETTING UP YOUR WEBSITE HOSTING

Now that you have secured your domain name, it's time to find a reliable web hosting provider that will serve as the home for your website. A web host provides the necessary server space and infrastructure to store your website's files and make it accessible to visitors worldwide. Follow these steps to quickly set up your website hosting using a cPanel-based provider:

1. Visit a reputable web hosting provider like www.vidahost.com. Choosing a reliable hosting provider is essential for the performance and security of your website. Look for a provider that offers cPanel-based hosting, as it provides a user-friendly interface for managing your website.

2. On the homepage of the hosting provider's website, you will typically find a range of hosting packages. Choose the package that suits your needs and budget. If you're just starting, it's often recommended to start with a basic shared hosting plan.

3. Register an account on the hosting provider's website and proceed with the payment process. Fill in the necessary details, including your contact information and billing information. Most hosting providers offer different billing cycles, such as monthly, yearly, or multi-year plans. Select the option that works best for you.

4. Once you have completed the registration and payment process, you will receive login credentials to access your hosting account. Log in to your account and locate the cPanel login page. The cPanel is a powerful control panel that allows you to manage various aspects of your website, including files, databases, email accounts, and more.

5. Enter your username and password to access the cPanel. You may need to navigate to a specific section or icon labeled "cPanel" or "Control Panel" to enter the management interface.

6. In your cPanel, you will find various options and features for managing your website. Look for an icon or section that allows you to add a new website or domain. This might be labeled as "Add New Website" or something similar. Click on this option and follow the instructions to associate your registered domain with your hosting account.

7. Once you have linked your domain to your hosting account, you may need to wait for a few minutes for the necessary configurations to take effect. This period allows the domain to propagate across the internet, making your website accessible.

8. After the waiting period, you can access your cPanel and start managing your website. Explore the different features available, such as file managers, email setup, database management, and more. Take some time to familiarize yourself with the cPanel interface and the tools it offers.

Remember, it's important to choose a reliable hosting provider that offers good performance, security, and customer support. While setting up your hosting is a relatively quick process, investing time in researching and selecting the right hosting provider will ensure a smoother experience for the long term.

Once your hosting is set up, you can begin uploading your website files, configuring email accounts, installing content management systems like WordPress, and exploring the various tools and features provided by your hosting provider.

LINKING YOUR DOMAIN TO YOUR WEB HOST

Now that you have your web address/domain and web hosting set up, it's time to connect them by configuring the DNS settings. This process ensures that when someone enters your web address in their browser, they will be directed to your website hosted on your chosen web host. Follow these instructions to link your domain to your web host:

Fast Approach for Namecheap:

1. Log in to your Namecheap account using your username and password.

2. Find the DNS SETTINGS page, usually accessible from your account dashboard or domain management section.

3. On the DNS SETTINGS page, you will see an option to choose between "Use Namecheap's NameServers" or "Use Custom NameServers." Select the "Use Custom NameServers" option.

4. Enter the first DNS name server address provided by your web host in the first line and the second DNS name server address in the second line.

5. Save the changes, and your domain will now be linked to your web host.

Fast Approach for GoDaddy:

1. Log in to your GoDaddy account using your username and password.

2. Go to the DOMAIN DETAILS page by clicking on the gear-wheel icon next to your domain and selecting "Domain Details."

3. In the DOMAIN DETAILS page, find the "Nameservers" section and click on "Manage."

4. In the pop-up window, select "Custom" as the setup type.

5. Add the two new name servers provided by your web host: "ns1.vidahost.com" and "ns2.vidahost.com." Remove any other name servers if they are listed.

6. Save the changes, and your domain will be linked to your web host.

Long Learning Approach:

1. Return to the website where you purchased your web address/domain, such as www.namecheap.com.

2. Sign in to your account on that website.

3. Navigate to the management area or settings section for your web address/domain. This might be labeled as "My Account" or something similar. Take your time to locate the appropriate section.

4. Look for an option to access the DNS settings or DNS setup, often referred to as "Domain Name Server" settings.

5. Open a new tab or window and search on Google for the name of your web host along with the term "nameserver." For example, search "vidahost nameserver."

6. Review the search results until you find descriptions that mention the name server addresses, typically starting with "ns1" (e.g., ns1.vidahost.com). Click on a relevant link that provides the name server addresses for your web host.

7. Copy the two name server addresses and return to the tab or window where you accessed the DNS settings or setup for your web address/domain.

8. Paste the copied name server addresses into the designated boxes, usually the first two boxes. For example, enter "ns1.vidahost.com" in the first box and "ns2.vidahost.com" in the second box.

9. Save the changes, and the DNS settings will be updated to link your domain to your web host.

After completing the DNS configuration, you need to create an FTP (File Transfer Protocol) account to manage your website files and upload them to the server. This process can typically be done through the cPanel provided by your hosting provider. Access the cPanel and look for an option to create an FTP account. Enter the necessary details, such as a username and password, and note down the FTP hostname provided by your hosting provider.

To transfer files to your hosting server, download and install FileZilla, a popular FTP client software. Open FileZilla and go to the "File" menu, then select "Site Manager." Click on "New Site" and give it a name. Enter the FTP hostname, username, and password you obtained earlier. Click "Connect," and FileZilla will establish a connection to your server.

From there, you can navigate to the relevant directories and upload your website files to the server using the drag-and-drop interface provided by FileZilla. This allows you to transfer your website files to the server and make them accessible to visitors.

By linking your domain to your web host and setting up the FTP account, you have successfully established the connection between your web address and your hosting provider. You are now ready to upload your website files and begin building your website.

SETTING UP EMAIL ACCOUNTS FOR YOUR DOMAIN

If you want to have professional email addresses associated with your domain (e.g., info@yourdomain.com), follow these steps to set up email accounts through your web hosting provider:

1. Log in to your web hosting control panel (cPanel) using the credentials provided by your hosting provider. This panel allows you to manage various aspects of your hosting account, including email settings.

2. Look for an option or section labeled "Email" or "Email Accounts" within the cPanel. Click on it to access the email management interface.

3. Choose the option to "Create New Email Account" or a similar command. You will be prompted to enter the desired email address and set a password for the account. Select a strong password to ensure the security of your email account.

4. Specify the storage quota for the email account. This determines the amount of disk space allocated to store the email messages. You can set a specific quota or choose an unlimited option, depending on your hosting plan and requirements.

5. Once you have entered the necessary information, click on the "Create" or "Add Account" button to create the email account. The system will generate the email address and associate it with your domain.

6. Repeat the process to create additional email accounts for other team members or purposes, if needed.

7. To access your email account, you can typically use a webmail interface provided by your hosting provider. Look for a link or button labeled "Webmail" within the email management section of your cPanel. Clicking on it will direct you to a web-based email client where you can log in with the email address and password you created.

8. Alternatively, you can set up your email accounts in an email client such as Microsoft Outlook, Apple Mail, or Mozilla Thunderbird. Use the provided email account details (email address, username, password, and server settings) to configure the email client according to its specific instructions.

By setting up email accounts associated with your domain, you can establish a professional and branded communication channel for your business or organization. This allows you to send and receive emails using email addresses that reflect your domain name.

Remember to regularly check and manage your email accounts, including configuring email forwarding, autoresponders, and spam filters, to ensure a smooth email communication experience.

Note: The exact steps and options for setting up email accounts may vary depending on your web hosting provider and the interface they offer. If you encounter any difficulties or have specific questions, refer to the documentation or support resources provided by your hosting provider, or reach out to their customer support for assistance.

IMPLEMENTING WEBSITE BACKUP AND SECURITY MEASURES

To safeguard your website and protect it from potential threats, it's crucial to implement backup and security measures. Follow these steps to ensure the security and integrity of your website:

1. Choose a Backup Solution: Look for backup options provided by your web hosting provider. They may offer automated backup services or tools that allow you to manually back up your website files and databases. Alternatively, you can explore third-party backup solutions or plugins specifically designed for your content management system (CMS) if applicable.

2. Set up Regular Backups: Determine a backup frequency that suits your needs, whether it's daily, weekly, or monthly. Schedule automated backups whenever possible to ensure consistent and reliable backups of your website files and databases. Configure the backup settings according to the instructions provided by your chosen backup solution.

3. Store Backups Securely: After performing backups, ensure that they are securely stored. Ideally, save backups in multiple locations, such as external hard drives, cloud storage services, or off-site backup solutions. This redundancy helps protect your data in case of any unforeseen circumstances.

4. Implement Security Measures: Enhance your website's security by taking proactive measures against potential threats. This includes:

    o Keeping Your CMS and Plugins Up to Date: Regularly update your CMS platform (e.g., WordPress,

Joomla) and installed plugins to benefit from security patches and bug fixes. Outdated software can make your website vulnerable to attacks.

o Using Strong Usernames and Passwords: Choose unique and complex usernames and passwords for your CMS admin panel, hosting account, and other relevant areas. Avoid common or easily guessable passwords and consider using a password manager to securely store your login credentials.

o Installing Security Plugins: Utilize security plugins or extensions provided by your CMS or reputable third-party security plugins. These tools can help monitor your website for potential vulnerabilities, block suspicious activities, and provide additional layers of protection.

o Enabling SSL (Secure Sockets Layer): Implement an SSL certificate on your website to secure data transmission and enable HTTPS encryption. Many hosting providers offer free SSL certificates through services like Let's Encrypt.

o Configuring Firewall and IP Whitelisting: Activate firewalls and consider implementing IP whitelisting to allow access only from trusted IP addresses. This helps restrict unauthorized access attempts to your website.

o Monitoring and Auditing: Regularly monitor your website's security logs and audit any suspicious activities. Look for unusual login attempts, file modifications, or other signs of potential breaches. You can utilize security plugins or server-level monitoring tools for this purpose.

Remember, website security is an ongoing effort. Stay informed about the latest security practices and vulnerabilities, and regularly review and update your security measures to stay ahead of potential threats.

By implementing backup and security measures, you can ensure the safety and integrity of your website, protecting it from data loss, cyber-attacks, and other security risks.

Note: The specific backup and security measures may vary depending on your web hosting provider, CMS platform, and the tools you choose to implement. Refer to the documentation and support resources provided by your hosting provider, CMS, or security plugin developers for detailed instructions and best practices.

REGULAR WEBSITE MAINTENANCE

To keep your website running smoothly and provide an optimal user experience, regular maintenance is essential. Follow these steps to establish a routine maintenance practice for your website:

1. Update Your CMS and Plugins: Stay up to date with the latest versions of your CMS platform (e.g., WordPress, Joomla) and installed plugins. Regularly check for updates and apply them to benefit from new features, security patches, and performance improvements. Many CMS platforms have built-in update functionality that allows you to easily update your website components.

2. Monitor Website Performance: Keep an eye on your website's performance to ensure it loads quickly and functions smoothly. Use tools like Google PageSpeed Insights or GTmetrix to analyze your website's speed and identify areas for improvement. Optimize images, enable caching, and minify code to enhance performance.

3. Review and Refresh Content: Regularly review the content on your website to ensure it remains relevant and engaging. Update outdated information, add new content, and remove any redundant or irrelevant material. Pay attention to grammar, spelling, and formatting to maintain a professional appearance.

4. Check for Broken Links: Broken links can negatively impact user experience and SEO. Use online tools or plugins to scan your website for broken links and fix them promptly. Update internal links whenever you make changes to your site structure or page URLs.

5. Backup Your Website: Regularly perform backups of your website files and databases to protect against data loss.

Create a backup schedule and ensure that backups are stored securely in different locations. Test the restoration process periodically to verify the integrity of your backups.

6. Monitor Security: Continuously monitor your website's security to identify and address any vulnerabilities. Consider using security plugins or services that provide malware scanning, firewall protection, and security audits. Stay informed about the latest security threats and follow best practices to safeguard your website.

7. Analyze Website Analytics: Utilize website analytics tools like Google Analytics to gain insights into your website's performance, visitor behavior, and traffic sources. Analyze data such as page views, bounce rate, and conversion rates to make informed decisions about improving your website's effectiveness.

8. Test Website Functionality: Regularly test your website's functionality across different devices, browsers, and screen sizes. Ensure that all links, forms, interactive elements, and media are working correctly. Fix any issues or inconsistencies that may arise during testing.

By incorporating regular website maintenance into your routine, you can ensure that your website remains functional, secure, and up to date. This helps provide a positive user experience, boost search engine rankings, and support your overall online presence.

Remember to allocate dedicated time for website maintenance and consider creating a checklist or calendar to stay organized and ensure no crucial tasks are overlooked.

Note: The specific maintenance tasks and tools may vary depending on your CMS platform, hosting environment, and specific website requirements. Refer to the documentation and resources provided by your CMS platform, hosting provider, and relevant plugins or services for detailed instructions and recommendations.

ENGAGE WITH YOUR WEBSITE VISITORS

To foster a sense of community and establish a strong connection with your website visitors, it's important to engage with them. Follow these steps to encourage interaction and build relationships with your audience:

1. Enable Comments and Feedback: If appropriate for your website, enable commenting functionality on your blog posts, articles, or other relevant sections. Encourage visitors to leave comments and provide feedback. Respond to comments promptly and engage in conversations to create a dialogue with your audience.

2. Social Media Integration: Integrate social media sharing buttons on your website to make it easy for visitors to share your content on their preferred social media platforms. Create profiles for your website on popular social media channels (e.g., Facebook, Twitter, Instagram) and actively engage with your followers. Respond to messages, comments, and mentions to foster two-way communication.

3. Email Newsletter: Offer an opt-in email newsletter to capture the contact information of interested visitors. Create compelling content and send regular newsletters with updates, exclusive offers, or valuable insights related to your website's niche. Encourage subscribers to provide feedback, ask questions, or share their experiences.

4. Interactive Content: Incorporate interactive elements into your website, such as quizzes, surveys, polls, or interactive infographics. These engage visitors and encourage them to participate actively. Capture their responses or opinions to gain valuable insights and tailor your content to their preferences.

5. Live Chat or Support: If feasible, consider implementing a live chat feature on your website. This allows visitors to ask questions or seek assistance in real-time. Respond promptly and provide helpful information to address their queries or concerns. Alternatively, offer a support email address or contact form for visitors to reach out to you.

6. Community Forums or Q&A Sections: If your website's niche lends itself to community interaction, consider creating a dedicated forum or Q&A section. This allows visitors to connect with each other, share knowledge, and seek answers to their questions. Moderate the community to ensure a positive and helpful environment.

7. User-Generated Content: Encourage visitors to contribute content to your website, such as guest blog posts, user testimonials, or user-submitted articles. Showcase and promote their contributions to foster a sense of involvement and recognition.

By actively engaging with your website visitors, you create a welcoming and interactive environment that encourages repeat visits, builds brand loyalty, and attracts new visitors through word-of-mouth referrals. Regularly monitor and respond to visitor interactions to maintain an ongoing relationship with your audience.

Remember, engagement requires consistent effort and genuine interaction. Be responsive, listen to feedback, and provide value to your visitors to create a positive and engaging user experience.

Note: The specific engagement strategies may vary depending on your website's niche, target audience, and the nature of your content. Tailor your engagement efforts to align with your website's goals and the preferences of your audience.

MEASURE AND ANALYZE WEBSITE PERFORMANCE

To assess the effectiveness of your website and make data-driven decisions for improvement, it's important to measure and analyze its performance. Follow these steps to gain insights into your website's performance and user behavior:

1. Set Up Web Analytics: Install a web analytics tool like Google Analytics on your website. Create an account, generate a tracking code, and add it to your website's code. This will enable you to collect data on website visitors, their behavior, traffic sources, and more.

2. Define Key Performance Indicators (KPIs): Determine the metrics that align with your website's goals. Common KPIs include website traffic, conversion rate, bounce rate, average session duration, and goal completions. Define specific targets or benchmarks for these KPIs to measure your website's performance effectively.

3. Analyze Traffic Sources: Explore the sources of your website traffic to understand how visitors find your website. Analyze data on organic search, direct traffic, referrals, social media, and paid advertising campaigns. This information will help you identify which channels are driving the most valuable traffic and where to focus your marketing efforts.

4. Track User Behavior: Dive into user behavior data to gain insights into how visitors navigate and interact with your website. Analyze metrics like page views, session duration, exit pages, and click-through rates. Identify popular pages, paths taken by visitors, and areas of the website that may require improvement.

5. Conduct Conversion Rate Analysis: Monitor and analyze your website's conversion rates to measure its effectiveness in achieving specific goals. Track conversions such as newsletter sign-ups, form submissions, purchases, or any other desired actions. Identify conversion bottlenecks and optimize the user experience to improve conversion rates.

6. Use Heatmaps and User Recording Tools: Utilize heatmapping and user recording tools to visualize user behavior and interactions on your website. Heatmaps show where users click, scroll, and spend the most time on a page. User recordings provide video recordings of actual user sessions, offering valuable insights into their browsing behavior and pain points.

7. A/B Testing and Conversion Optimization: Implement A/B testing to experiment with different versions of your website elements, such as headlines, call-to-action buttons, or layout variations. Test these changes with a portion of your website visitors to determine which version performs better in terms of your defined KPIs. Implement the winning version to optimize your website's performance.

8. Generate Reports and Review Regularly: Set up automated reports to receive regular updates on your website's performance. Review the reports periodically and analyze trends, patterns, and opportunities for improvement. Use the insights gained to make data-driven decisions for optimizing your website's performance and user experience.

By measuring and analyzing your website's performance, you gain valuable insights into its strengths, weaknesses, and opportunities for improvement. Use this information to make informed decisions, implement targeted optimizations, and continuously enhance your website's effectiveness.

Note: The specific analytics tools and techniques may vary depending on the web analytics platform you choose and any additional tools you utilize for heatmapping, user recordings, or A/B testing. Familiarize yourself with the documentation and resources provided by these tools to make the most of their features and capabilities.

DOUBLING UP WEBSITE SECURITY

To protect your website and its valuable data from cyber threats and maintain the trust of your visitors, it's crucial to implement robust security measures. Follow these steps to enhance the security of your website:

1. Keep Software Up to Date: Regularly update your website's CMS, plugins, themes, and other software components to ensure you have the latest security patches and bug fixes. Outdated software can be vulnerable to attacks, so staying up to date is essential.

2. Use Strong Passwords: Use strong, unique passwords for all your website accounts, including the CMS, hosting, and email accounts. Avoid using easily guessable passwords and consider using a password manager to securely store and generate complex passwords.

3. Implement SSL Encryption: Secure your website with SSL (Secure Socket Layer) encryption to protect data transmitted between your website and visitors. This is particularly important if you collect sensitive information such as passwords, payment details, or personal data. Obtain an SSL certificate from a trusted certificate authority and configure your website to use HTTPS.

4. Install a Web Application Firewall (WAF): A WAF can help protect your website from common security threats, such as malicious bots, DDoS attacks, and SQL injections. Consider using a WAF plugin or a cloud-based WAF service to add an additional layer of security to your website.

5. Regularly Backup Your Website: Create regular backups of your website's files and databases. Store backups securely in off-site locations, such as cloud storage or external

drives. In the event of a security breach or data loss, having recent backups ensures you can restore your website quickly.

6. Use Secure Hosting: Choose a reputable hosting provider that prioritizes security. Look for features such as robust server security measures, regular system updates, and proactive monitoring for potential threats. Research hosting providers and read reviews to ensure they have a strong security track record.

7. Monitor and Audit User Accounts: Regularly review user accounts on your website and remove any inactive or unnecessary accounts. Limit user privileges and assign roles with appropriate access levels to minimize the risk of unauthorized access or malicious activities.

8. Implement Captcha and Anti-Spam Measures: Use CAPTCHA (Completely Automated Public Turing test to tell Computers and Humans Apart) to prevent automated bots from submitting forms or sending spam. Consider using anti-spam plugins or services to reduce the amount of unwanted comments or contact form submissions.

9. Educate Yourself and Your Team: Stay informed about the latest security best practices and threats in the web development and cybersecurity communities. Educate yourself and your team on topics such as secure coding practices, phishing awareness, and password hygiene. Regularly review and update security policies and guidelines for your website.

By implementing these security measures, you can significantly reduce the risk of security breaches, data loss, and other malicious activities on your website. Maintaining a secure website not only protects your own interests but also instills confidence in your visitors, helping to build trust and credibility.

Note: The specific security measures and tools may vary depending on your website's CMS platform, hosting environment, and additional security services you choose to implement. Stay informed about the latest security trends and consult with security experts or professionals for guidance specific to your website's needs.

WORDPRESS VS JOOMLA: CHOOSING THE RIGHT CMS FOR YOUR WEBSITE

When it comes to building your website, selecting the right Content Management System (CMS) is crucial. The CMS you choose will determine the ease of use, flexibility, and functionality of your website. Two popular CMS options that have gained widespread popularity are WordPress and Joomla. Let's delve deeper into these platforms to help you make an informed decision that suits your website needs.

WordPress: WordPress is the world's most widely used CMS, and it's known for its user-friendly interface and extensive plugin and theme ecosystem. If you're primarily focused on creating a blog or a simple website with a few additional pages, WordPress is an excellent choice. It offers a straightforward setup process, a wide range of professionally designed themes, and a vast selection of plugins that extend the functionality of your website. WordPress is perfect for individuals, bloggers, small businesses, and even larger organizations that want to create and regularly update content, whether it's blog posts, articles, images, or videos. With its intuitive dashboard and a wealth of resources available online, WordPress allows you to quickly get your website up and running with minimal technical knowledge.

Joomla: Joomla is another popular CMS that caters to users who require more advanced features and a higher degree of customization. It offers greater flexibility and scalability, making it suitable for websites with a larger scale and complexity. With Joomla, you can create websites with extensive content hierarchies, multiple user registration forms, interactive community features, e-commerce functionality, and much more. It provides a robust framework for building complex websites and allows you to manage a wide range of content types efficiently.

Joomla is an excellent choice for businesses, organizations, or individuals who require advanced content management capabilities, user interactions, and multimedia management. While Joomla may have a steeper learning curve compared to WordPress, it offers more flexibility in terms of website structure and management.

Ease of Use: WordPress is known for its user-friendly interface and intuitive content management system. It offers a simplified dashboard that allows even beginners to quickly set up and manage their website. With a vast library of themes and plugins, WordPress provides an extensive range of options to customize your website without any coding knowledge. On the other hand, Joomla has a steeper learning curve, requiring a bit more technical proficiency. It offers more advanced customization options and flexibility but may take some time to fully understand and navigate.

Content Management: Both WordPress and Joomla excel at content management, but they approach it differently. WordPress is primarily built for blogging and content-driven websites. It offers a seamless experience for creating, organizing, and publishing blog posts and articles. With its built-in blogging features and user-friendly editor, WordPress makes it easy to manage and update your content. Joomla, on the other hand, is more versatile and allows for the creation of complex websites with hierarchical content structures. It offers robust content management capabilities, making it suitable for websites with extensive content, such as news portals, online magazines, and corporate websites.

Flexibility and Customization: Joomla provides more flexibility and customization options compared to WordPress. It offers a sophisticated framework that allows you to create intricate website structures and implement advanced functionalities. With Joomla, you have greater control over user permissions, access levels, and content organization. It's an excellent choice for websites that require user registrations, memberships, or extensive e-commerce functionality. WordPress, while not as flexible as Joomla, still offers a wide range of themes and plugins that allow for significant customization of your website's design and functionality. It's an ideal choice for individuals and small businesses who want a user-friendly CMS with a vast plugin ecosystem.

Community Support and Updates: Both WordPress and Joomla have large and active communities of users and developers. This means that you'll have access to a wealth of resources, tutorials, forums, and support communities. WordPress has a larger user base, which translates to a more extensive plugin and theme library. It also receives regular updates and security patches. Joomla, while having a slightly smaller user base, still offers a strong community support system and frequent updates to ensure optimal performance and security.

Ultimately, the choice between WordPress and Joomla depends on your specific website requirements, technical expertise, and long-term goals. WordPress is an excellent choice for bloggers and individuals looking for a user-friendly CMS with a vast ecosystem of themes and plugins. Joomla, on the other hand, suits those who need more advanced functionality, customization options, and scalability.

Take the time to evaluate your needs, explore the features and capabilities of both CMS options, and consider your comfort level with the learning curve. Both WordPress and Joomla have their strengths and can provide a solid foundation for building your website.

WordPress: To quickly get started with WordPress, you'll first need to install it on your web host. This can be done by following the step-by-step guide provided by the WordPress website. The installation process is straightforward and can be completed in a few simple steps.

Once you have WordPress installed, it's important to familiarize yourself with its features and functionalities. Explore the WordPress dashboard and learn how to create and publish posts, add media, customize the appearance with themes, and extend functionality with plugins. The WordPress website provides comprehensive documentation and tutorials to help you navigate and make the most of the platform.

To enhance the design of your WordPress website, you can choose from a wide range of professional themes. These themes offer pre-designed layouts and customizable options to create a visually appealing and unique website. The WordPress Theme Directory is a great resource to browse and select themes that suit your style and purpose.

Joomla: To begin your journey with Joomla, you'll need to download the latest version of Joomla from the official Joomla website. Once downloaded, you can follow the installation instructions provided by Joomla to set it up on your web host.

After the installation, take some time to explore the Joomla administration interface. Familiarize yourself with the different sections, such as content management, user management, menu creation, and extension installation. Joomla offers a comprehensive user guide on their website, which can help you understand and navigate the various features of the CMS.

To customize the design of your Joomla website, you can choose from a variety of templates available in the Joomla Extension Directory. These templates provide different styles and layouts, allowing you to create a visually appealing website that aligns with your brand or niche.

Remember, both WordPress and Joomla have active communities and forums where you can seek assistance, find tutorials, and connect with other users. Take advantage of these resources to deepen your understanding and make the most of these powerful CMS platforms.

By following these quick-start guides for WordPress and Joomla, you'll have a solid foundation to create and manage your website. Whether you choose WordPress for its user-friendly interface and vast plugin ecosystem or Joomla for its robust features and extensibility, you'll be on your way to building a successful online presence.

To sum it up:

- WordPress is an ideal choice for small to simple medium websites, particularly those focused on blogging or content-driven websites. It's user-friendly, easy to set up, and offers a vast selection of themes and plugins.

- Joomla is well-suited for websites of all sizes, from small to large, and offers more advanced features and customization options. It provides greater flexibility for managing various content types and implementing complex functionalities.

When making your decision, consider the scale and complexity of your website, your specific content management needs, and your level of technical expertise. Both WordPress and Joomla have active communities, extensive documentation, and a wide range of resources available to support you in building and maintaining your website. Take the time to explore and familiarize yourself with the features, support, and capabilities of each CMS to determine which one aligns best with your website goals.

RECAP WORDPRESS

Creating a website with WordPress is a straightforward process that can be broken down into several key steps. Here is a simplified explanation of how to create a website using WordPress:

Step 1: Choose a Domain Name and Web Hosting Start by selecting a domain name for your website – this is the web address that people will use to access your site (e.g., www.yourwebsite.com). Once you've chosen a domain name, sign up for a web hosting service that will provide the server space to store your website's files and make it accessible on the internet.

Step 2: Install WordPress Most web hosting providers offer a one-click WordPress installation option. After logging into your hosting account, find the WordPress installer and follow the instructions to install WordPress on your domain. This process will create the necessary database and set up the initial configuration for your website.

Step 3: Choose and Customize a Theme WordPress offers a wide range of free and premium themes that determine the overall design and layout of your website. Choose a theme that aligns with your website's purpose and customize it by adjusting colors, fonts, and other visual elements. You can also upload your own logo and customize the header, footer, and widget areas.

Step 4: Install Essential Plugins WordPress plugins add extra functionality to your website. Some essential plugins to consider include a caching plugin to improve website performance, an SEO plugin to optimize your site for search engines, a security plugin to protect against threats, and a contact form plugin to allow visitors to get in touch with you. Install and configure these plugins to enhance your website's functionality.

Step 5: Create Pages and Content Start building your website by creating pages such as Home, About, Services, and Contact. WordPress uses a block-based editor called Gutenberg, which allows you to easily add and arrange different content blocks like text, images, videos, and more. Customize each page's content and design to suit your needs. Additionally, you can create a blog section to regularly publish articles or updates.

Step 6: Configure Website Settings Navigate to the WordPress settings section to configure important website settings such as site title, tagline, permalink structure, and reading options. This is where you can specify how your website's URLs will appear and set whether your homepage will display a static page or the latest blog posts.

Step 7: Add Functionality with Additional Plugins If there are specific features or functionalities you want on your website, search for relevant plugins in the WordPress Plugin Directory. Whether you need an e-commerce solution, a membership system, or a gallery, there are plugins available to extend your website's capabilities. Install and configure these plugins according to your requirements.

Step 8: Customize Menus and Navigation Create a navigation menu that enables visitors to easily navigate your website. You can add pages, categories, custom links, or even external links to your menu. Define the menu structure and order, and assign it to the appropriate location in your theme. This will ensure your visitors can find the information they need.

Step 9: Optimize Your Website for SEO Utilize an SEO plugin to optimize your website for search engines. Configure meta tags, titles, and descriptions for each page to improve your website's visibility in search engine results. Focus on keyword research, relevant content, and proper use of headings to enhance your SEO efforts.

Step 10: Regularly Update and Maintain Your Website Keep your website up to date by regularly updating WordPress, themes, and plugins to ensure security and compatibility. Also, regularly create backups of your website's files and database to safeguard against any potential data loss.

Remember, this is a simplified explanation of the process, and creating a website with WordPress may require more detailed steps depending on your specific needs and preferences.

Here are some handy tricks and tips to enhance your experience with WordPress:

Use Keyboard Shortcuts: WordPress offers several keyboard shortcuts to speed up your workflow. For example, press "Alt + Shift + H" to see the available shortcuts or use "Ctrl + S" to save changes when editing a post or page.

Enable Distraction-Free Writing: When writing content in the WordPress editor, click on the "Fullscreen" mode button (located in the top-right corner) to enter distraction-free writing mode. This provides a clutter-free interface, allowing you to focus solely on your writing.

Utilize Custom Post Types: WordPress allows you to create custom post types, which are different content structures beyond just regular posts and pages. You can create custom post types for portfolios, testimonials, products, and more, providing flexibility in organizing and presenting your content.

Explore Page Builders: Page builder plugins like Elementor, Divi, or Beaver Builder offer drag-and-drop interfaces for creating stunning and complex page layouts without coding. They provide pre-designed templates, widgets, and customization options, making it easier to design visually appealing pages.

Optimize Images: Large image files can slow down your website. To optimize images, use plugins like Smush or ShortPixel to compress and optimize images without sacrificing quality. Additionally, consider using the "lazy loading" technique to load images as users scroll down the page, improving page load times.

Utilize Categories and Tags: Properly categorize and tag your posts to improve navigation and SEO. Categories help organize content into broad topics, while tags offer more specific descriptors. Consistent and relevant categorization and tagging will make it easier for visitors to find related content.

Customize Permalinks: Ensure your website's permalinks (URL structure) are SEO-friendly and user-friendly. In the WordPress dashboard, go to "Settings" > "Permalinks" to customize the structure. Choose a format that includes the post name or category, making it easier for search engines and visitors to understand the content of the page.

Enable Comments Moderation: To prevent spam comments, enable comment moderation. In the WordPress dashboard, go to "Settings" > "Discussion" and check the box to require manual approval of comments before they appear on your site. You can also install plugins like Akismet to automatically filter spam comments.

Schedule Content: WordPress allows you to schedule posts in advance. When creating or editing a post, click on the "Publish" button, and in the "Publish" meta box, choose the desired date and time for publication. This feature is useful for planning and maintaining a consistent posting schedule.

Regularly Update WordPress, Themes, and Plugins: Keeping your WordPress core, themes, and plugins up to date is crucial for security and performance. Update them regularly to access new features, bug fixes, and security patches. Backup your website before performing updates for added precaution.

OTHER CMS OPTIONS

When it comes to choosing a Content Management System (CMS) for your website, WordPress and Joomla are not the only options available. There are numerous other CMS platforms that cater to different website needs and preferences. Let's explore 100 other CMS options that you can consider for your website:

1. Drupal: A flexible and robust CMS known for its scalability and security features.

2. Magento: A powerful CMS specifically designed for e-commerce websites, offering extensive e-commerce functionality.

3. Shopify: An all-in-one platform that simplifies the creation and management of online stores.

4. Squarespace: A user-friendly CMS that provides beautiful templates and drag-and-drop functionality for easy website building.

5. Wix: A popular website builder that offers a wide range of templates and customization options.

6. Joomla: An advanced CMS suitable for creating complex websites with multiple functionalities and user interactions.

7. Ghost: A minimalist and lightweight CMS designed specifically for bloggers and content creators.

8. Typo3: A feature-rich CMS with advanced enterprise-level capabilities and a strong focus on security.

9. Concrete5: A user-friendly CMS that combines ease of use with powerful editing and customization features.

10. SilverStripe: A flexible CMS with a modular architecture that allows for easy customization and extensibility.

11. ExpressionEngine: A highly customizable CMS that offers flexibility for building various types of websites.

12. MODX: A content-focused CMS that emphasizes flexibility, scalability, and customization options.

13. Craft CMS: A developer-friendly CMS with a focus on flexibility, performance, and content management.

14. ProcessWire: A powerful and flexible CMS known for its simplicity and developer-friendly environment.

15. Umbraco: An open-source CMS that provides a flexible and scalable platform for building websites and web applications.

16. Contao: A user-friendly CMS that offers extensive features for creating and managing websites.

17. Grav: A flat-file CMS that prioritizes speed, simplicity, and ease of use.

18. Bolt: A lightweight and easy-to-use CMS that focuses on simplicity and speed.

19. Textpattern: A flexible and extensible CMS that emphasizes ease of use and content management.

20. October CMS: A Laravel-based CMS that provides a modern and intuitive platform for building websites and web applications.

21. dotCMS: An enterprise-level CMS that offers robust content management and personalization features.

22. Pimcore: A flexible and scalable CMS with built-in digital asset management and e-commerce capabilities.

23. Radiant CMS: A simple and elegant CMS with a focus on ease of use and clean code.

24. Microweber: A drag-and-drop CMS that allows for easy website building and content management.

25. Gravwell: A headless CMS that separates the content creation process from the presentation layer, enabling greater flexibility.

26. Publii: A desktop-based CMS that offers simplicity and security for managing static websites.

27. Jekyll: A static site generator that allows for the creation of fast and secure websites.

28. Hugo: Another popular static site generator known for its speed and simplicity.

29. Netlify CMS: A Git-based CMS that integrates seamlessly with the JAMstack architecture.

30. Cockpit: A self-hosted CMS that provides a simple and flexible platform for managing content.

31. GetSimple CMS: A lightweight CMS that focuses on simplicity and ease of use.

32. Pagekit: A modern and lightweight CMS that offers a user-friendly interface and extensibility.

33. Ghost CMS: A headless CMS that enables developers to build custom front-end experiences while managing content.

34. Orchard Core: A modular CMS built on the ASP.NET Core framework, providing flexibility and extensibility.

35. Kirby: A file-based CMS that offers simplicity, flexibility, and a clean user interface.

36. Strapi: An open-source headless CMS that allows developers to create powerful API-driven websites and applications.

37. Directus: An open-source headless CMS with a focus on simplicity and extensibility.

38. ApostropheCMS: A developer-friendly CMS built on Node.js that offers content management capabilities.

39. Plone: An open-source CMS built on Python that emphasizes security and scalability.

40. Wagtail: A user-friendly CMS built on Django that offers a streamlined editing experience.

41. Locomotive CMS: A flexible and scalable CMS with a focus on user experience and performance.

42. ButterCMS: A headless CMS that provides a content API for easy integration with any front-end technology.

43. Prismic: A headless CMS that offers a GraphQL API for content management and delivery.

44. Sanity: A real-time, collaborative CMS that allows teams to work together on content creation and management.

45. Storyblok: A headless CMS that offers a visual editor and flexible content delivery options.

46. Netlify: A powerful hosting and CMS platform that enables seamless website deployment and content management.

47. Strikingly: A website builder and CMS that focuses on simplicity and mobile responsiveness.

48. Webflow: A visual CMS and website builder that allows for easy design and customization.

49. Sitecore: An enterprise-level CMS that offers advanced personalization and marketing automation features.

50. Kentico: A feature-rich CMS with a focus on content management, e-commerce, and digital marketing.

These are just a few examples of the many CMS options available to suit different website needs and preferences. Each CMS has its unique features, strengths, and target audiences. Take the time to research and explore these options to find the CMS that best aligns with your website goals and requirements.

THE POWER OF CMS + SEO

Whether you've chosen WordPress or Joomla as your content management system (CMS), these powerful tools will help you unlock the full potential of your website and attract organic traffic.

WordPress:

1. Google Analyticator: Google Analyticator is a valuable tool that allows you to track your website's traffic, understand referral sources, and analyze user behavior. This information will help you optimize your content and improve the overall user experience. By knowing which pages are receiving the most visits and how visitors navigate through your site, you can make data-driven decisions to enhance engagement and conversion rates. Follow this video tutorial to install and configure Google Analyticator: Video Tutorial: Installing Google Analyticator on WordPress

2. Google XML Sitemap Generator: Creating an XML sitemap is crucial for search engines to understand the structure of your website and index it effectively. The Google XML Sitemap Generator plugin automatically generates a sitemap for your WordPress site, making it easier for search engines to crawl and index your content. This improves your website's visibility in search engine results and increases the chances of attracting organic traffic. Watch this video tutorial to learn how to install and activate the plugin: Video Tutorial: Installing Google XML Sitemap Generator on WordPress

3. Yoast SEO: Yoast SEO is a powerful plugin that helps you optimize your content for search engines. It provides real-time analysis and suggestions while you write your articles, ensuring that your content is well-optimized for search

visibility. Yoast SEO helps you craft compelling meta titles and descriptions, optimize keyword usage, and improve readability. The plugin also offers advanced features for XML sitemap generation, social media integration, and more. Install Yoast SEO by following this video tutorial: Video Tutorial: Installing Yoast SEO on WordPress. For a deeper understanding of how to use Yoast SEO effectively, watch this video tutorial: Video Tutorial: Using Yoast SEO for WordPress

Joomla:

1. Asynchronous Google Analytics: Asynchronous Google Analytics is a powerful tool that helps you track your website's traffic, understand referral sources, and analyze user behavior. By integrating Google Analytics with your Joomla website, you can gain valuable insights into visitor demographics, behavior flow, and conversion rates. This information allows you to make data-driven decisions and optimize your website's performance. Install and configure Asynchronous Google Analytics by following this video tutorial: Video Tutorial: Installing Asynchronous Google Analytics on Joomla

2. XMap: XMap is an extension that generates XML sitemaps for your Joomla website. XML sitemaps help search engines understand the structure and content of your site, leading to better indexing and improved search visibility. With XMap, you can easily create and update XML sitemaps to ensure that search engines can discover and crawl all your important pages. You can find and install XMap from the official Joomla Extensions Directory or through this link: XMap Extension for Joomla. Learn how to use XMap by watching this video tutorial: Video Tutorial: Using XMap for Joomla

3. SEO: Joomla is a more advanced CMS, and effective SEO requires a deeper understanding of its features. In addition to using plugins, it's essential to implement proper on-page optimization, such as optimizing meta tags, heading tags, and content structure. This video tutorial provides insights into performing SEO effectively with Joomla, including keyword research, content optimization, and website structure: Video Tutorial: SEO Best Practices for Joomla

By implementing these SEO strategies and using the recommended plugins for your chosen CMS, you'll enhance your website's visibility in search engine rankings and attract more organic traffic. Remember, SEO is an ongoing process, and it's important to regularly monitor your website's performance, make adjustments, and stay up-to-date with the latest SEO practices.

Now, armed with these SEO tools and techniques, you're ready to optimize your website and unlock its full potential in the digital landscape. Good luck on your SEO journey!

EMAIL MARKETING

One of the key aspects of growing your online presence is building an email list of individuals who are genuinely interested in the topics you will be writing about. By following these steps, you can create a high-quality email list before even publishing your first article or post:

1. Reach out to Friends: Start by informing your friends about your website and the topics you will be covering. If they show interest, ask for their email addresses to include them in your list.

2. Utilize Facebook Groups: Join relevant groups on Facebook and connect with 15-20 people per day who share an interest in your chosen topics. Engage in conversations and inquire if they would like to be notified about your upcoming articles. Request their email addresses if they express interest. Remember, you can also approach individuals individually outside of groups.

3. Tap into Your Professional Network: Explore if any colleagues or contacts within your organization or business share an interest in the content you will be providing. If they do, inquire if they would like to receive updates when your articles are published and collect their email addresses.

4. Attend Meetups and Events: Visit meetups, events, and social gatherings that attract individuals who might be interested in your chosen areas or topics. Share information about your website and your intentions to write articles in those areas. If they demonstrate interest, kindly ask for their email addresses.

5. Leverage Twitter: Create a Twitter account and regularly tweet about your key areas of interest. Share articles, provide insights, and engage with your audience. Limit your following to a manageable number and gradually increase your tweeting frequency. After a month, aim to tweet seven times a day, including retweets, mentions of your website or articles, and links to subscribe to your newsletter. This video tutorial offers guidance on using Twitter effectively: <u>Video Tutorial: How to Use Twitter</u>

6. Engage on LinkedIn: Join relevant groups on LinkedIn and reach out to 10-50 individuals each day who share an interest in your chosen areas or topics. Introduce them to your website or upcoming articles and ask if they would like to receive updates. Request their email addresses or provide a link to subscribe. This video tutorial provides insights on using LinkedIn effectively: <u>Video Tutorial: How to Use LinkedIn</u>

7. Participate in Forums: Identify four forums where your key topics or areas of interest are actively discussed. Ensure each forum has a substantial membership base of at least 1000 members. Register an account and engage in discussions on a regular basis, spending no more than 40 minutes per day across all forums. After a few weeks, inquire within the forums about creating a signature or directly ask members for guidance. Include a link to your website or newsletter subscription in your signature. Contact 4-7 people each day and inquire if they would be interested in subscribing. Additionally, contribute useful forum posts every 14 days that solve problems or offer valuable insights. Understanding the basics of forums can be learned from this video tutorial: <u>Video Tutorial: Understanding Forum Usage</u>

By actively implementing these strategies, you can gradually build a robust email list filled with individuals who are genuinely interested in your content and eager to receive updates from you. Remember, it's essential to maintain consistent engagement and provide valuable information to keep your subscribers engaged and interested in your future content.

Email marketing is a powerful tool that allows you to directly connect with your audience, build relationships, and drive engagement. Here are some techniques and a list of popular email marketing software to consider:

1. Building an Effective Email List:

    o   Use opt-in forms on your website to capture visitor emails.

    o   Offer incentives, such as exclusive content or discounts, in exchange for email sign-ups.

    o   Segment your email list based on demographics, interests, or engagement levels to personalize your messaging.

2. Creating Engaging Email Content:

    o   Craft compelling subject lines to grab the recipient's attention.

    o   Use a conversational tone and make your emails easy to read.

    o   Include visually appealing elements like images, videos, and infographics.

    o   Provide valuable and relevant content that educates, entertains, or solves a problem.

    o   Incorporate strong calls to action (CTAs) to encourage desired actions from recipients.

3. Automation and Personalization:

   o   Utilize automation tools to send targeted emails triggered by specific actions or behaviors.

   o   Personalize your emails by addressing recipients by name and tailoring content to their preferences.

   o   Implement drip campaigns to nurture leads over time and guide them through the buyer's journey.

4. A/B Testing and Analytics:

   o   Test different email elements, such as subject lines, CTAs, or email layouts, to optimize engagement.

   o   Analyze email performance metrics, including open rates, click-through rates, and conversions.

   o   Use the insights gained from testing and analytics to refine your email marketing strategies.

5. Email Marketing Software:

   o   Mailchimp: Offers a user-friendly interface, automation features, and customizable email templates.

   o   Constant Contact: Provides easy-to-use tools for creating, sending, and tracking email campaigns.

   o   GetResponse: Offers advanced automation capabilities, landing page creation, and webinar hosting.

   o   AWeber: Provides a range of email marketing features, including autoresponders and list segmentation.

- o Campaign Monitor: Offers drag-and-drop email builder, advanced analytics, and personalized customer journeys.

- o ConvertKit: Designed for creators, it offers features like customizable opt-in forms and subscriber tagging.

Remember to comply with email marketing regulations, such as obtaining permission from subscribers and providing an option to unsubscribe in every email. Regularly monitor your email performance and adjust your strategies based on recipient engagement to maximize the effectiveness of your email marketing campaigns.

PUBLISHING CONTENT & MANAGEMENT

When it comes to publishing website content, it's important to create engaging articles that provide value to your readers. Here are some tips and resources to help you in this process:

1. Optimal Word Count and Image Usage:

   o Aim for articles with a word count between 500-1000 words to provide comprehensive and informative content.

   o Include at least one relevant image for every 400-500 words to enhance visual appeal and engagement.

   o High-quality and visually appealing images can be sourced from websites offering free copyright images such as the ones listed below:

      ▪ Inc.com Free Stock Photos

      ▪ Websitefromscratch.org Free Royalty-Free Images

      ▪ Bufferapp.com Free Image Sources

2. Consistent Article Posting Frequency:

   o Strive to publish at least one article or post every 7-14 days to keep your website updated and maintain engagement with your audience.

   o Regularly providing fresh content signals to search engines that your website is active and relevant.

3. Incorporating Social Share Icons:

- Include social share icons within your articles to encourage readers to share your content on social media platforms.

- Twitter, Google+, and Facebook share icons are popular choices, but you can customize the selection based on your target audience and their preferred social networks.

- Sharing your content on social media platforms helps to increase visibility and attract more visitors to your website.

- For WordPress, you can use a plugin like <u>WordPress Social Sharing Plugin</u> to easily add social share icons to your articles.

- For Joomla, you can check out the <u>Sharing Buttons</u> extension/plugin for adding social share icons.

4. Leveraging Social Signals:

- Social signals, such as likes, shares, and comments on social media platforms, can positively impact your search engine rankings.

- Encourage readers to share your articles by creating valuable and shareable content.

- Engage with your audience on social media to foster discussions and increase the likelihood of social signals.

- Remember that social signals may have a short-term impact, so it's important to consistently produce high-quality content to maintain search engine visibility.

Remember to track the performance of your articles using analytics tools, such as Google Analytics, to gain insights into visitor behavior, engagement, and conversions. This data can help you refine your content strategy and make informed decisions to optimize your website's performance.

Keep in mind that the resources and techniques mentioned in this section are focused on website content creation and promotion. It's important to comply with ethical and legal guidelines, such as respecting copyright laws, obtaining proper permissions, and adhering to platform-specific terms of service for social media promotion.

ere are additional techniques and a list of popular email marketing software to further expand on the topic of email marketing:

Techniques for Email Marketing:

1. Opt-in Forms: Place opt-in forms strategically on your website to capture visitors' email addresses. Offer incentives such as free e-books, exclusive content, or discounts to encourage sign-ups.

2. Segmentation: Divide your email list into segments based on demographics, interests, or past interactions. This allows you to send targeted and personalized emails that resonate with each group.

3. Drip Campaigns: Set up automated drip campaigns to send a series of pre-scheduled emails to subscribers over a specific time period. This helps nurture leads and guide them through the customer journey.

4. Personalization: Address subscribers by their first name and tailor your content to their preferences and behaviors. Personalized emails have higher open and click-through rates.

5. A/B Testing: Test different subject lines, email layouts, call-to-actions, and content to optimize your email campaigns. Analyze the results and make data-driven decisions for better performance.

6. Mobile Optimization: Ensure your emails are mobile-friendly and responsive to provide a seamless experience for subscribers who access their emails on smartphones or tablets.

7. Email Automation: Utilize automation tools to trigger emails based on specific actions or events, such as welcome emails, abandoned cart reminders, or birthday greetings.

Popular Email Marketing Software:

1. Mailchimp: A widely used email marketing platform that offers a user-friendly interface, email templates, marketing automation, and advanced analytics.

2. Constant Contact: Provides email marketing tools, customizable templates, list management features, and event registration services.

3. AWeber: Offers a comprehensive suite of email marketing features, including drag-and-drop email builders, automation workflows, subscriber segmentation, and analytics.

4. GetResponse: Provides a range of email marketing features, including autoresponders, landing page builders, webinar hosting, and advanced segmentation capabilities.

5. Campaign Monitor: Offers customizable email templates, drag-and-drop email builders, automation workflows, and real-time analytics.

6. ConvertKit: Designed for bloggers and content creators, ConvertKit provides features for building email lists, creating automated email sequences, and managing subscriber tags.

7. HubSpot: An all-in-one marketing platform that includes email marketing tools, CRM integration, lead nurturing capabilities, and advanced analytics.

Remember to choose an email marketing software that aligns with your specific needs, budget, and technical requirements. It's essential to comply with email marketing regulations, such as obtaining proper consent from subscribers and providing an easy way to unsubscribe from your email list.

By implementing effective email marketing techniques and leveraging reliable software, you can build a strong connection with your audience, drive engagement, and achieve your marketing goals.

WORDPRESS TEMPLATES

There are several reputable marketplaces where you can purchase WordPress templates, also known as themes. These marketplaces offer a wide range of options, including free and premium themes. Here are some popular platforms where you can buy WordPress templates:

ThemeForest (https://themeforest.net/) ThemeForest is one of the largest marketplaces for WordPress themes. It offers a vast selection of professionally designed themes across various categories. Each theme is thoroughly reviewed for quality and includes detailed documentation and support from the theme authors.

Elegant Themes (https://www.elegantthemes.com/) Elegant Themes is a renowned provider of premium WordPress themes and plugins. They offer a membership-based model where you can access their entire collection of themes and plugins, including the popular Divi theme and Divi Builder plugin.

StudioPress (https://www.studiopress.com/) StudioPress is known for its Genesis Framework, a powerful foundation for WordPress themes. They offer a collection of premium themes built on the Genesis Framework, which are highly optimized for performance and SEO.

TemplateMonster (https://www.templatemonster.com/) TemplateMonster provides a wide range of WordPress themes and templates for various purposes. They offer both free and premium options, with a focus on delivering visually appealing and feature-rich designs.

MOJO Marketplace (https://www.mojomarketplace.com/) MOJO Marketplace offers a diverse selection of WordPress themes, plugins, and other digital products. They feature a curated collection of both free and premium themes from various authors.

Creative Market (https://creativemarket.com/) Creative Market is a platform where independent designers and creators sell their digital products, including WordPress themes. It offers a wide range of unique and creative themes for different niches and styles.

When purchasing a WordPress theme, make sure to read user reviews, check the theme's compatibility with your WordPress version, and review the features and support provided by the theme authors. Additionally, consider themes that are regularly updated and have good documentation to assist you in setting up and customizing your website.

Remember, always purchase themes from reputable sources to ensure quality, security, and ongoing support for your WordPress website.

To install WordPress themes from marketplaces like ThemeForest, Elegant Themes, StudioPress, TemplateMonster, MOJO Marketplace, or Creative Market, you can follow these general steps:

Purchase and download the theme: After selecting and purchasing a theme from the marketplace, you will usually receive a downloadable zip file. Save this file to your computer.

Log in to your WordPress dashboard: Open your WordPress website's admin area by entering your website URL followed by

"/wp-admin" (e.g., www.yourwebsite.com/wp-admin). Log in with your credentials.

Go to the Themes section: In the WordPress dashboard, navigate to "Appearance" and click on "Themes." This will take you to the Themes page where you can manage and install themes.

Upload the theme: Look for an "Add New" or "Upload Theme" button. Click on it to access the theme upload functionality. Choose the downloaded zip file of the theme from your computer and click on the "Install Now" button.

Activate the theme: After the theme is successfully uploaded, click on the "Activate" button to make it the active theme for your website.

Configure theme settings: Some themes may have specific settings or customization options. Review the theme documentation provided by the author for instructions on how to configure the theme and make any desired changes.

Install recommended plugins: Some themes may require specific plugins to unlock certain features or functionality. The theme documentation will usually provide details on any recommended or required plugins. Install and activate the recommended plugins as instructed.

Import demo content (optional): If the theme provides demo content, you may have the option to import it to quickly set up your website with sample content. Refer to the theme documentation for instructions on how to import the demo content.

Customize the theme: Customize your newly installed theme to match your branding and preferences. Edit the site title, logo, colors, fonts, and other design elements through the theme's customization options or the WordPress Customizer.

Remember to regularly update the installed theme, along with WordPress core and plugins, to ensure compatibility and security. Updates can be found under the "Themes" or "Updates" section in the WordPress dashboard.

Here are a few additional considerations and tips when installing WordPress themes:

Review Theme Documentation: Take the time to read the theme documentation provided by the author. It often includes detailed instructions on theme installation, customization options, recommended plugins, and troubleshooting guidance. Familiarize yourself with the documentation to make the most of your chosen theme.

Ensure Theme Compatibility: Before purchasing a theme, check its compatibility with your version of WordPress. Verify that the theme is regularly updated by the author to ensure it remains compatible with the latest WordPress updates.

Choose a Responsive Theme: Opt for a responsive theme that adapts to different screen sizes and devices. This will ensure your website looks good and functions properly on desktops, tablets, and mobile devices.

Consider Page Builders: If you prefer a more visual and flexible approach to designing your website, choose a theme that is compatible with popular page builder plugins like Elementor, Divi, or Beaver Builder. These plugins allow you to create and customize complex page layouts using a drag-and-drop interface.

Check Theme Reviews and Ratings: Before purchasing a theme, review user ratings and comments on the marketplace. This feedback can provide insights into the quality, performance, and support offered by the theme author.

Keep Your Theme Lightweight: Opt for lightweight themes that are optimized for speed and performance. Avoid themes that come bundled with excessive features or unnecessary code, as they can impact your website's loading time.

Backup Your Website: Before making any major changes to your website, including installing a new theme, always perform a backup of your website files and database. This ensures you have a restore point in case anything goes wrong during the installation or customization process.

Seek Support if Needed: If you encounter any issues or have questions during the installation or customization of your theme, reach out to the theme author's support team or consult the marketplace's support resources. They are there to assist you and provide guidance when needed.

The appearance and functionality of your website can be greatly influenced by the chosen theme. Take the time to select a theme that aligns with your goals, offers the desired features, and suits your design preferences. With careful consideration and proper installation, your chosen WordPress theme can help you create a visually appealing and functional website.

GETTING HIGH QUALITY BACKLINKS

Obtaining high-quality backlinks is essential for improving your website's search engine rankings and increasing its visibility. Follow these steps to acquire valuable backlinks from reputable blogs and websites:

1. Identify Relevant Blogs/Websites: Conduct a Google search to find 12 blogs or websites that focus on topics related to your chosen niche. Ensure that the selected sites meet the following criteria:

   o Minimum Page Rank (PR) of 4

   o Minimum Page Authority (PA) of 40

   o Minimum MozRank of 4

2. Verify Page Metrics: Use tools such as bulkseotools.com to check the PR, moonsy.com/domain_authority/ for PA, and moonsy.com/mozrank/ for MozRank. Insert the URLs of the blogs or websites to determine if they meet the desired metrics.

Note: If you encounter limitations in accessing these tools due to IP restrictions, consider using the TOR browser for anonymous surfing. This browser changes your IP address, allowing you to use the tools without limitations. Watch this video tutorial on how to download and use the TOR browser: http://www.youtube.com/watch?v=fxJ7VT5Epcs.

3. Engage through Comments: Start engaging with the blog's community by regularly commenting on their articles. Provide valuable insights, respond to other comments, and compliment the author's work. Maintain this activity for at least one month to establish a rapport with the author and other readers.

4. Contact the Author: After building a relationship, reach out to the author and ask if they would be willing to mention your article or website on their platform. Explain the relevance and value of your content. This short video provides insights on how to approach authors for backlinks: http://www.youtube.com/watch?v=pqe7U4YOGOA.

5. Repeat the Process: Once you have secured backlinks from the first set of blogs, find another 12 relevant blogs and repeat the process. Maintain communication with the previous authors to strengthen relationships and explore opportunities for further backlinks. You can consider including links to the author's articles within your own content to foster mutual collaboration.

6. Guest Blogging: Guest posting is another effective strategy for acquiring backlinks. Approach blog owners and propose writing an article to be published on their platform. This allows you to showcase your expertise to a new audience and earn valuable backlinks. Learn more about guest blogging in this video: http://www.youtube.com/watch?v=3F73CTsDcUY.

Optional: Utilize Yahoo! Answers: Yahoo! Answers can be a source of additional traffic and backlinks. Create accounts on Yahoo! Answers and follow this approach:

- Post a relevant question from one account.

- Answer the question after two days using another account and include a link to your website.

- Rate your own answer as the best after three days to ensure it remains visible.

- This pattern helps create a natural appearance and generates traffic, even though the links are no-follow.

Yahoo! Answers has a large user base, providing opportunities for exposure. Learn more about this strategy in the book 'Grey Hat SEO.'

By implementing these techniques, you can gradually build a network of high-quality backlinks, enhancing your website's authority and search engine visibility. Remember to prioritize relevancy and maintain genuine engagement with the blog community to foster long-term relationships.

Expanding on the topic of acquiring high-quality backlinks, let's delve deeper into some effective techniques and explore a few popular email marketing software options:

1. Create Link-Worthy Content: To attract authoritative websites and blogs for backlinks, focus on creating high-quality, informative, and engaging content. Develop articles, blog posts, infographics, or videos that provide unique insights, valuable information, or solve specific problems within your niche. Link-worthy content naturally attracts attention and encourages other websites to reference and link back to your site.

2. Outreach to Industry Influencers: Identify influential individuals within your industry who have a strong online presence and a significant following. Reach out to them and offer to collaborate on content creation or request a feature on their platforms. Influencers' endorsements and backlinks can significantly boost your website's credibility and visibility.

3. Guest Blogging: Guest blogging involves writing articles for other websites within your industry. Look for authoritative blogs that accept guest contributions and offer to write informative and relevant articles for their audience. In return, you can include a backlink to your website in the

author bio or within the article itself. Guest blogging helps establish your expertise, expands your reach, and earns valuable backlinks from reputable sources.

4. Broken Link Building: Identify websites within your niche that have broken links on their pages. Reach out to the website owners or webmasters, inform them about the broken links, and suggest your relevant content as a replacement. This mutually beneficial approach helps the website owner fix broken links while providing you with an opportunity to secure a valuable backlink.

5. Social Media Promotion: Leverage social media platforms to promote your content and attract attention from potential backlink sources. Share your articles, blog posts, or videos on platforms like Twitter, LinkedIn, Facebook, and Instagram, tagging relevant industry influencers or websites. Engage with the community, respond to comments, and encourage sharing of your content, which can lead to natural backlinks.

6. Email Outreach: Identify websites, blogs, or online publications within your industry that may be interested in your content. Craft personalized outreach emails introducing yourself, your website, and the value your content provides. Propose collaboration opportunities such as guest blogging, expert interviews, or content features. Personalized and well-targeted email outreach can yield positive responses and valuable backlinks.

Popular Email Marketing Software:

1. Mailchimp: Mailchimp is a widely used email marketing platform that offers a user-friendly interface, customizable email templates, automation features, and robust analytics. It allows you to design and send professional-looking

emails, manage subscriber lists, and track campaign performance. Mailchimp offers both free and paid plans, making it suitable for businesses of all sizes.

2. ConvertKit: ConvertKit is an email marketing tool designed specifically for bloggers and content creators. It offers features such as customizable email templates, automated email sequences, subscriber tagging, and advanced audience segmentation. ConvertKit focuses on simplicity and provides actionable analytics to help you optimize your email marketing campaigns.

3. AWeber: AWeber is a comprehensive email marketing solution that offers a wide range of features, including drag-and-drop email builders, automation workflows, audience segmentation, and analytics. It provides pre-built email templates and allows integration with popular website platforms and e-commerce tools. AWeber offers flexible pricing plans based on the size of your subscriber list.

4. GetResponse: GetResponse is an all-in-one marketing platform that includes email marketing, landing page creation, marketing automation, and webinar hosting. It offers a user-friendly interface, responsive email templates, advanced automation features, and robust analytics. GetResponse provides a range of pricing plans based on the size of your subscriber list and additional features required.

5. Resource Page Link Building: Identify websites or blogs that have resource pages listing helpful links and references within your niche. Reach out to the website owners and suggest your content as a valuable addition to their resource page. If your content aligns well with their page's theme and provides value to their audience, they may include a link to your website.

6. Competitor Backlink Analysis: Analyze the backlink profiles of your competitors to identify opportunities for acquiring similar backlinks. Use tools like Ahrefs, SEMrush, or Moz to identify the websites linking to your competitors' sites. Reach out to these websites and pitch your content as a valuable resource that complements the existing backlinks.

7. HARO (Help a Reporter Out): Sign up for HARO, a platform that connects journalists and bloggers with expert sources. HARO sends daily emails with inquiries from reporters seeking expert opinions or quotes for their articles. Respond to relevant inquiries and provide valuable insights. If your response gets featured, you'll earn a backlink from the publication.

8. Influencer Collaboration: Collaborate with industry influencers, bloggers, or content creators to co-create content or participate in interviews. This collaborative content can be published on both your website and the influencer's platform, providing valuable backlinks and exposure to their audience.

9. Testimonials and Reviews: Provide testimonials or reviews for products, services, or tools that you use within your industry. Reach out to the companies or websites and offer to share your positive feedback. In return, they may feature your testimonial on their website, including a backlink to your site.

10. Local Business Directories: If you have a local business, ensure that you are listed in relevant local business directories. These directories often provide an opportunity to include a backlink to your website. Submit accurate and consistent information about your business to improve your online presence and local search rankings.

11. Content Syndication: Identify reputable websites or platforms that accept content syndication. Syndicating your content allows it to be republished on other websites, providing you with exposure to a wider audience and potential backlinks. Ensure that the republished content includes a canonical link back to the original article on your website to avoid any duplicate content issues.

12. Internal Linking: Don't forget the power of internal linking within your own website. Link relevant pages and articles together to guide users through your content and provide search engines with a clear hierarchy and understanding of your site's structure. Effective internal linking helps distribute link equity across your website and improves user navigation.

Remember, building high-quality backlinks takes time and effort. Focus on creating valuable content, fostering relationships with industry influencers, and implementing effective outreach strategies to gradually acquire authoritative backlinks that will enhance your website's visibility and organic search rankings.

THE POWER OF WEBSITE MANAGEMENT

Whether you're a beginner or have some experience, this guide will walk you through the essential steps to create a successful online presence. Let's get started!

PART 1: Getting Started

1. Define Your Website's Purpose: Clearly identify the purpose and goals of your website. Determine the target audience and the content you plan to provide.

2. Choose a Domain Name: Select a domain name that reflects your brand and is memorable. Register your domain name through a reliable registrar like Namecheap or GoDaddy.

3. Web Hosting Selection: Choose a reputable web hosting provider that meets your website's requirements. Consider factors like reliability, speed, security, and customer support.

4. Set Up Your Website: Install a Content Management System (CMS) to manage and publish your website's content. WordPress and Joomla are popular choices, offering different features based on your needs.

PART 2: Website Design and Development

5. Design Your Website: Select a professional template or theme for your CMS that aligns with your brand's identity. Customize the design elements and layout to create a visually appealing website.

6. Create Engaging Content: Craft high-quality content that is valuable, informative, and relevant to your target audience. Focus on articles with a word count of 500-1000 words and incorporate images to enhance engagement.

7. Search Engine Optimization (SEO): Optimize your website for search engines by using tools like Yoast SEO (WordPress) or SEO extensions (Joomla). Pay attention to keyword research, on-page optimization, meta tags, and URL structure.

8. Social Media Integration: Integrate social media share icons into your website to encourage content sharing. Utilize plugins or extensions specific to your CMS platform for seamless integration.

PART 3: Driving Traffic and Building Backlinks

9. Email Marketing: Build an email list by collecting contacts from interested individuals. Use opt-in forms and incentives to encourage sign-ups. Leverage email marketing software like Mailchimp or ConvertKit to manage and automate your campaigns.

10. High-Quality Backlinks: Focus on acquiring backlinks from authoritative websites in your niche. Research and reach out to relevant blogs and websites with a good PageRank (PR) and Page Authority (PA). Engage with their content and establish relationships to earn backlinks.

11. Content Promotion: Share your articles and website content on social media platforms like Twitter, Facebook, and LinkedIn. Engage with your audience, join relevant groups, and participate in discussions to increase visibility and drive traffic.

12. Guest Blogging: Write guest posts for other blogs within your industry. Approach website owners with a pitch that showcases your expertise and offers value to their audience. Guest blogging can earn you backlinks and expose your brand to a wider audience.

13. Online Directories: Submit your website to relevant online directories and local business listings. Ensure accurate and consistent information across directories to improve your online presence and local search rankings.

14. Content Syndication: Explore opportunities to syndicate your content on reputable platforms or websites. Syndication exposes your content to a wider audience, potentially earning backlinks and increasing brand visibility.

15. Engage in Online Communities: Participate in forums, groups, and question-answer platforms related to your niche. Contribute valuable insights, answer questions, and provide helpful information. Establish yourself as an authority and include links to your website when appropriate.

PART 4: Analyzing and Improving

16. Website Analytics: Set up Google Analytics to track website performance, user behavior, and traffic sources. Analyze data regularly to gain insights and make data-driven decisions to improve your website's performance.

17. Conversion Rate Optimization (CRO): Implement strategies to improve user experience, increase conversions, and achieve your website's goals. Test elements like headlines, call-to-action buttons, and page layouts to optimize conversions.

18. Continuous Improvement: Regularly update and refresh your website's content to keep it relevant and engaging. Stay updated with industry trends and best practices to refine your strategies and adapt to changes in the digital landscape.

PART 5: Monetization and Website Maintenance

19. Monetization Strategies: Explore various monetization methods to generate revenue from your website. Consider options such as display advertising, affiliate marketing, sponsored content, selling products or services, or creating a membership site. Research and choose the monetization strategy that aligns with your website's goals and audience.

20. E-commerce Integration: If you plan to sell products or services on your website, set up an e-commerce platform. Popular e-commerce solutions include WooCommerce (WordPress) and VirtueMart (Joomla). Configure your online store, set up payment gateways, and ensure a smooth and secure checkout process.

21. Website Security: Protect your website and its data by implementing security measures. Install security plugins or extensions, enable SSL certificates to secure user data, regularly update CMS and plugins, and perform backups to safeguard against potential threats or data loss.

22. Website Performance Optimization: Optimize your website for speed and performance. Compress images, enable caching, minify CSS and JavaScript files, and use a content delivery network (CDN) to enhance loading times. A fast-loading website improves user experience and search engine rankings.

23. Mobile Responsiveness: Ensure your website is mobile-friendly and responsive across different devices and screen sizes. Test your website's responsiveness using tools like Google's Mobile-Friendly Test and make necessary adjustments to provide a seamless user experience on mobile devices.

24. User Engagement and Feedback: Encourage user engagement by enabling comments on your articles or

incorporating a discussion forum. Respond to user comments and feedback promptly to build a sense of community and foster a loyal audience.

25. Continuous Learning and Adaptation: Stay updated with the latest trends, technologies, and SEO practices in the ever-evolving digital landscape. Follow industry blogs, attend webinars, and join relevant communities to expand your knowledge and adapt your strategies accordingly.

26. Regular Website Maintenance: Regularly update your CMS, themes, and plugins to ensure compatibility and security. Monitor website performance, fix broken links, and conduct periodic content audits to maintain a well-functioning and up-to-date website.

27. Website Growth and Expansion: As your website gains traction and authority, explore opportunities to expand your online presence. Consider diversifying your content formats (videos, podcasts), launching a YouTube channel, or leveraging social media platforms to reach a wider audience.

28. Analyze and Refine: Continuously monitor website analytics, track key performance metrics, and analyze user behavior to identify areas for improvement. Utilize data-driven insights to refine your content, marketing strategies, and user experience.

Remember, building and maintaining a successful website is an ongoing process. Stay committed to creating valuable content, engaging with your audience, and adapting to changes in the digital landscape. With dedication and persistence, your website has the potential to grow and thrive.

FINAL WORD

Congratulations on embarking on your journey to create a remarkable website! By following the steps outlined in this guide, you have equipped yourself with valuable knowledge and actionable strategies to build a successful online presence. As you venture forward, remember that success in the digital world is not achieved overnight. It requires dedication, perseverance, and a commitment to delivering exceptional value to your audience.

Creating a website is just the beginning. To truly stand out in the digital landscape, it is important to continually expand your knowledge and refine your skills. The world of online marketing and web development is ever-evolving, and staying ahead of the curve is key to staying relevant.

To further enhance your understanding and expand your skill set, I recommend exploring the following reading materials:

1. "The Art of SEO" by Eric Enge, Rand Fishkin, Jessie C. Stricchiola, and Stephan Spencer - This comprehensive guide delves into the intricacies of search engine optimization, providing valuable insights and techniques to improve your website's visibility and rankings. Dive deep into keyword research, on-page optimization, link building, and more.

2. "Content Rules: How to Create Killer Blogs, Podcasts, Videos, Ebooks, Webinars (and More) That Engage Customers and Ignite Your Business" by Ann Handley and C.C. Chapman - This book offers practical advice on creating compelling content that captivates your audience and drives meaningful engagement. Learn how to develop a content strategy, craft persuasive storytelling, and leverage various content formats to connect with your target audience.

3. "Influence: The Psychology of Persuasion" by Robert B. Cialdini - Understanding the principles of persuasion is essential for effective marketing. This book explores the psychology behind influencing people's behavior and provides insights into building persuasive strategies. Discover how to leverage social proof, scarcity, authority, and other psychological triggers to drive action and engagement.

4. "Epic Content Marketing: How to Tell a Different Story, Break through the Clutter, and Win More Customers by Marketing Less" by Joe Pulizzi - Learn the art of content marketing and how to create remarkable, shareable content that attracts and retains a loyal audience. Explore strategies for finding your unique voice, developing a content mission statement, and distributing your content effectively.

5. "Don't Make Me Think: A Common Sense Approach to Web Usability" by Steve Krug - Usability is a crucial aspect of website design. This book offers practical advice on creating intuitive and user-friendly websites that enhance the overall user experience. Gain insights into user behavior, usability testing, and designing for accessibility.

Content Marketing:

1. "Content Rules: How to Create Killer Blogs, Podcasts, Videos, Ebooks, Webinars (and More) That Engage Customers and Ignite Your Business" by Ann Handley and C.C. Chapman

2. "Epic Content Marketing: How to Tell a Different Story, Break through the Clutter, and Win More Customers by Marketing Less" by Joe Pulizzi

3. "They Ask You Answer: A Revolutionary Approach to Inbound Sales, Content Marketing, and Today's Digital Consumer" by Marcus Sheridan

4. "Content Inc.: How Entrepreneurs Use Content to Build Massive Audiences and Create Radically Successful Businesses" by Joe Pulizzi

5. "The Content Code: Six Essential Strategies to Ignite Your Content, Your Marketing, and Your Business" by Mark W. Schaefer

Social Media Marketing:

1. "Jab, Jab, Jab, Right Hook: How to Tell Your Story in a Noisy Social World" by Gary Vaynerchuk

2. "Social Media Marketing All-in-One For Dummies" by Jan Zimmerman and Deborah Ng

3. "Influence: The Psychology of Persuasion" by Robert B. Cialdini

4. "Crushing It!: How Great Entrepreneurs Build Their Business and Influence—and How You Can, Too" by Gary Vaynerchuk

5. "Contagious: How to Build Word of Mouth in the Digital Age" by Jonah Berger

Email Marketing:

1. "Email Marketing Rules: A Step-by-Step Guide to the Best Practices that Power Email Marketing Success" by Chad White

2. "Email Marketing Demystified: Build a Massive Mailing List, Write Copy that Converts and Generate More Sales" by Matthew Paulson

3. "Email Persuasion: Captivate and Engage Your Audience, Build Authority and Generate More Sales With Email Marketing" by Ian Brodie

4. "The Rebel's Guide to Email Marketing: Grow Your List, Break the Rules, and Win" by DJ Waldow and Jason Falls

5. "Email Marketing: An Hour a Day" by Jeanniey Mullen and David Daniels

6.

Pay-Per-Click Advertising (PPC):

1. "Ultimate Guide to Google AdWords" by Perry Marshall, Mike Rhodes, and Bryan Todd

2. "Advanced Google AdWords" by Brad Geddes

3. "PPC Mastery: The Ultimate Guide to Paid Advertising" by Stefan James

4. "Conversion Optimization: The Art and Science of Converting Prospects into Customers" by Khalid Saleh and Ayat Shukairy

5. "The Complete Guide to Facebook Advertising" by Brian Meert

Influencer Marketing:

1. "Influencer: Building Your Personal Brand in the Age of Social Media" by Brittany Hennessy

2. "The Influencer Code: How to Unlock the Power of Influencer Marketing" by Amanda Russell

3. "The Age of Influence: The Power of Influencers to Elevate Your Brand" by Neal Schaffer

4. "Influencer Marketing For Dummies" by Kristy Sammis, Cat Lincoln, and Stefania Pomponi

5. "The Influencer Marketing Blueprint: How to Build Brand Awareness, Drive Sales, and Grow Your Business with Influencer Marketing" by Shane Barker

Mobile Marketing:

1. "The Art of Mobile Persuasion: How the World's Most Influential Brands Are Transforming the Customer Relationship through Courageous Mobile Marketing" by Jeff Hasen

2. "Mobile Marketing: Winning Strategies for Today's Mobile-First Consumer" by Daniel Rowles

3. "Mobile Marketing: How Mobile Technology is Revolutionizing Marketing, Communications and Advertising" by Daniel Rowles

4. "Mobile Marketing: Strategy, Implementation and Practice" by Adele Gritten and Ian Chaston

5. "The Mobile Marketing Handbook: A Step-by-Step Guide to Creating Dynamic Mobile Marketing Campaigns" by Kim Dushinski

Analytics and Data-Driven Marketing:

1. "Web Analytics 2.0: The Art of Online Accountability and Science of Customer Centricity" by Avinash Kaushik

2. "Data-Driven: Creating a Data Culture" by Hilary Mason and DJ Patil

3. "Predictive Analytics: The Power to Predict Who Will Click, Buy, Lie, or Die" by Eric Siegel

4. "Big Data Marketing: Engage Your Customers More Effectively and Drive Value" by Lisa Arthur

5. "Marketing Analytics: Data-Driven Techniques with Microsoft Excel" by Wayne L. Winston

Inbound marketing:

1. "Inbound Marketing: Attract, Engage, and Delight Customers Online" by Brian Halligan and Dharmesh Shah

2. "Content Chemistry: The Illustrated Guide to Content Marketing" by Andy Crestodina

3. "The New Rules of Marketing and PR: How to Use Content Marketing, Podcasting, Social Media, AI, Live Video, and Newsjacking to Reach Buyers Directly" by David Meerman Scott

4. "They Ask, You Answer: A Revolutionary Approach to Inbound Sales, Content Marketing, and Today's Digital Consumer" by Marcus Sheridan

5. "Inbound Content: A Step-by-Step Guide to Doing Content Marketing the Inbound Way" by Justin Champion

Influencer marketing:

1. "Influence: The Psychology of Persuasion" by Robert Cialdini

2. "The Age of Influence: The Power of Influencers to Elevate Your Brand" by Neal Schaffer

3. "The Influencer Code: How to Unlock the Power of Influencer Marketing" by Amanda Russell

4. "Influencer: Building Your Personal Brand in the Age of Social Media" by Brittany Hennessy

5. "The Ultimate Guide to Influencer Marketing: Step-by-Step
    Strategies, Templates, and Tools for Leveraging the Power
    of Influencer Marketing" by Joe Sinkwitz

Remember, building a successful website is an ongoing process.
Continuously seek new knowledge, stay updated with industry
trends, and adapt your strategies accordingly. Embrace the
challenges and setbacks along the way as opportunities for growth
and improvement. With passion, dedication, and a commitment to
delivering exceptional value, your website has the potential to
make a profound impact in the online world.

Best of luck on your journey to digital success!